1/17

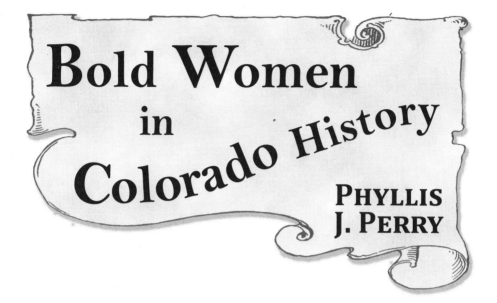

Bold Women
in
Colorado History

PHYLLIS
J. PERRY

2012
Mountain Press Publishing Company
Missoula, Montana

Library of Congress Cataloging-in-Publication Data

Perry, Phyllis Jean.
 Bold women in Colorado history / Phyllis J. Perry.
    p. cm.
 Includes bibliographical references and index.
 ISBN 978-0-87842-584-6 (pbk. : alk. paper)
 1. Women—Colorado—Biography—Juvenile literature.
 2. Women—Colorado—History—Juvenile literature.
 3. Colorado—Biography—Juvenile literature. I. Title.
 CT3262.C6P47 2012
 920.7209788—dc23
                          2011046971

PRINTED IN THE UNITED STATES

MP Mountain Press
PUBLISHING COMPANY
P.O. Box 2399 • Missoula, MT 59806 • 406-728-1900
800-234-5308 • info@mtnpress.com
www.mountain-press.com

*For Clare, Julia, and Emily, the next generation
of Bold Women in Colorado and beyond*

Contents

Acknowledgments

The author is indebted to Marie Des Jardin, Mary Peace Finley, Claudia Mills, Annie Nagda, Leslie O'Kane, and Elizabeth Wrenn for their constant support and their insightful suggestions for this book. I am also indebted to Sarah Everhart of History Colorado and Coi Drummond-Gehrig of the Denver Public Library for their assistance in locating images for this book. A special thanks goes to my dedicated editor, Gwen McKenna, for her careful and detailed work on the manuscript.

INTRODUCTION

The ten bold women included in this book are remarkable in the impact they have made on history in Colorado and far beyond. Some were poor; some were wealthy. They influenced spheres of life from entertainment to social work, from medicine to literature. Each faced unique challenges. In meeting these challenges they were indeed bold: venturesome, daring, radical, confident, and intrepid.

Our first biography looks at Clara Brown. Born a slave, she watched as her family was sold and taken away from her, but she eventually bought her freedom and headed west. Making her way as a laundress and cook, she reached out to others along the way, endearing her to many, and persisted against extreme odds to find her lost daughter. Next we meet Isabella Bird, world traveler, author, and photographer, who shared her journeys and insights through her writings and photos. The story of her climb up Longs Peak in the autumn of 1873 with the colorful Jim Nugent as her guide became a popular book that convinced many to make the trek to see the spectacular country that became Rocky Mountain National Park.

Augusta Tabor left her sheltered life in the East to follow her husband to Colorado. More than once, she found herself the only white woman in wild western mining towns. She helped her husband become a silver king, only to be thrown aside, yet she still found a way to survive. A well-known figure in Colorado is Indian peacemaker Chipeta. She was born a Kiowa Apache but grew up with the Utes and married a chief. She guided her husband through difficult decisions in a time when the U.S. government was forcing radical changes on the lives of Native Americans.

Mary Elitch Long left her home in California as a teenage bride. With her husband, she created the fantastic Elitch Gardens in Denver. This magical place offered not only gorgeous gardens, but also wild animals, live entertainment, and carnival rides. Even after the deaths of two husbands, she persisted, becoming a respected businesswoman. The life of Margaret "Molly" Brown is an American legend, full of myth but also truth. Many of the stories of her childhood are fiction, and she was never called Molly in her lifetime, but her move from mining camp to Denver society, her leadership of the survivors of the shipwrecked *Titanic*, and her dedication to humanity are indisputable facts.

Another extraordinary Coloradoan was Emily Griffith, a dedicated teacher who found a way to make education available not only to youngsters, but also to adults, including immigrants and working people, expanding the limits of education forever. Around the same time, medical pioneer Justina Ford changed the way Colorado looked at health care. When she received her medical license in Denver in 1902, Justina became the first African American female doctor in the state of Colorado. It was the beginning of a long career of service to poor and immigrant families that included delivering 7,000 babies. Josephine Roche was born into a life of privilege, but she was unwavering in her efforts to help the poor, new immigrants, and struggling coal miners socially and economically. Finally we meet Mary Coyle Chase, a flamboyant reporter and a caring wife and mother who touched the hearts of millions with her whimsical play about an invisible rabbit.

These ten bold women represent only a fraction of women who influenced lives in Colorado and around the world. At various times in history and in diverse situations, they provided proof of the enormous influence that can be wielded by one woman.

Clara Brown, circa 1875 to 1880 —Courtesy Western History Collection, Denver Public Library

1

CLARA BROWN

Angel of the Rockies

Clara Brown watched in stony silence as her ten-year-old daughter, in a pink gingham dress, stood on the auction block. Trembling and wide-eyed, little Eliza Jane stared over at her mother, her eyes pleading; but there was nothing Clara could do. It was the summer of 1836, County Court Day in Russellville, Kentucky, when farmers and their families came into town from great distances to buy and sell goods. Everything was for sale: livestock, farm tools, cookware, cloth, furniture, harnesses, food staples—and slaves. People crowded in around the low, wooden platform to get a good look at the merchandise. Buyers signaled their bids with a nod of the head or a pull of the earlobe.

Thirty slaves were to be sold today. Potential buyers had already come up and examined the slaves, checking their teeth and feeling the muscles of their arms and legs. Clara, her husband, her son, and her two daughters were all up for sale, to be auctioned off one by one. Now, as Eliza Jane stood before the crowd, the heat, the tension, and the fear built up until she was overcome. Right then and there, Eliza Jane threw up. The auctioneer was concerned, not because the child was upset but because he was worried that the vomiting might lower the girl's price.

After she was sold, with no chance to say goodbye to her mother, Eliza Jane was loaded onto a wagon along with other purchases—

a sack of grain, a butter churn. Clara, too, was sold, to a man she'd never met. And so began her new life, still a slave and now without knowing where her children were or what would become of them. Someday, perhaps, she would find them. Someday, perhaps, she would be free.

Clara Brown was born into slavery in Spotsylvania, Virginia, probably in January 1800. The exact date of her birth is unknown because at that time no one bothered to keep records of the birth of slave children. Slaves did not even have their own last name; they were simply given the surname of their master. In Clara's case, she took the last name of her third owner, George Brown.

When she was three years old, Clara and her mother were sold to Ambrose Smith, a tobacco farmer in Fredericksburg, Virginia. Luckily, the Smiths proved to be compassionate owners, and Clara spent the next six years on their farm. When the family decided to move to Kentucky in 1809, they took their slaves with them. With five other families in a small wagon train, the Smiths followed the Wilderness Road, a treacherous path through the Appalachian Mountains created by Daniel Boone and his men in 1775. Sometimes the travelers had to stop and make rafts to get their wagons across rivers, or tie ropes to the wagons to pull them up steep hills. Along the way they watched anxiously for hostile natives, though Clara's mother, who was part Cherokee, professed not to fear Indians.

When they finally reached Logan County, Kentucky, in May 1809, Clara and her mother thought they had arrived in paradise. The Smiths had chosen a piece of land near Big Muddy Creek, and the country was beautiful. The men cleared the fields and built a farmhouse, some barns, a milk house with a waterwheel over the creek, and a row of cabins for the slaves. While the men worked in the fields, Clara's mother did the cooking and laundry and milked the cows. Even the children helped. Clara and the two Smith boys collected and piled up brush, which was then burned for fertilizer.

Before long, Clara was helping her mother with various household tasks. She not only fed the chickens but also killed them, plucked them, and turned them into dinner. She washed clothes and pressed them with a heavy iron heated on the wood-burning stove. Clara knew how to do just about everything—sewing, shoe repair, baking, canning, gardening, and nursing the sick.

Mrs. Smith was especially kind to Clara and her mother, taking them to church and teaching Clara to read a little, though she risked some punishment by doing so, since it was illegal to educate slaves. In 1918, Clara married a fellow slave named Richard, and the Smiths threw them a wedding dinner. Richard and Clara had four children—Richard Junior, Margaret, and twin girls Paullina Ann and Eliza Jane.

In 1834 Clara suffered two great blows, and another one struck just two years later. First, her mother died. Then, in a terrible accident, little Paullina drowned in the river as her twin sister, Eliza Jane, looked on helplessly. In a final tragedy, the kindly Mr. Smith died in 1836, and his family, unable to continue farming without him, sold everything—the farm, the equipment, and, yes, even the slaves. Thus was Clara sold to George Brown, a hat maker who ran a shop in Russellville.

Working as a house servant in the Brown home, Clara wore a fancy starched white apron and cap when she served the family at the table. She worked hard, and the Browns were kind. When Clara told them about her family members being sold to different bidders, they made an effort to find out what had happened to them. Clara's husband and son, it was thought, were taken to a large cotton plantation some distance away, and they were never heard from again. But her daughters, Margaret and Eliza Jane, were known to be with families in the area. Although she could not see them, Clara occasionally caught news of her girls. Eventually she heard that Margaret had died of a respiratory illness. As the years passed, Clara tried to keep track of Eliza Jane, but by the early 1850s she could no longer find any information about her only surviving daughter and had no idea of her whereabouts.

In 1856 Mr. Brown died, and Clara was to be sold once again. But Brown had made a surprising stipulation in his will. He left to Clara the sum of $300, enough for her to buy her "freedom papers." The legal conditions of her freedom required that she had to leave the state of Kentucky within one year, or she would again be classified as a slave.

For the next year, Clara worked for Mr. Brown's two daughters, who paid her a salary. She saved every penny she could. In 1857, her year was up and she had to leave Kentucky. With the money she had saved, plus what was left of her inheritance, Clara took a flat-boat to St. Louis, Missouri, where a friend of the Brown family lived. In addition to her freedom papers, she carried a letter of reference from the Brown sisters in which they described her talents and her deep sense of honor.

Missouri, a slave state, was not the safest destination for a newly freed slave. Upon her arrival in St. Louis, Clara went straight to the home of the Browns' friend, a German merchant named Jacob Brunner, with her letter of reference. The Brunners hired Clara to work in their home six days a week, cleaning, cooking, and sewing. While in their employ, she learned to prepare German foods. On Sundays, her day off, Clara attended a German Methodist church in St. Louis, sitting in the section reserved for "colored" people. For the rest of the day, she questioned people at the river docks, trying to pick up news of Eliza Jane.

Clara had not been in St. Louis very long when the financial panic of 1857 struck, affecting the economy of the entire country. Facing hard times in St. Louis, the Brunner family decided to try their luck in Kansas Territory, and Clara went with them. Kansas, not yet a state, was in conflict at this time as pro- and antislavery factions fought to win control of the region. The proslavery element made Kansas a dangerous place for newly freed slaves. It was common for mercenaries to kidnap free blacks, destroy their freedom papers, and sell them into slavery again in Missouri.

Clara and the Brunners settled in Fort Leavenworth, where Clara joined the First Missionary Baptist Church, an all-black congregation. It was here that she met Becky Johnson, a freed slave from Kentucky, who made her living running a laundry service. The two became close friends.

When the Brunners decided to move once again, this time to California, Clara stayed behind. With her friend Becky's help, she opened her own laundry service, and she earned enough to support herself. In her spare time, Clara continued to seek out news of Eliza Jane, but she never found anyone who knew anything about her daughter. Clara did not lose faith, however.

In 1858, a gold discovery in the Rocky Mountains triggered a gold rush, and Clara guessed that her daughter might have gone farther west to the new goldfields. In the spring of 1859, she decided to go to Colorado, then part of Utah Territory, to look for Eliza Jane. Hearing of a wagon train that was about to leave on the two-month trip to Denver, Clara approached the train master, Col. Benjamin Wadsworth, and offered him a deal. In exchange for transportation, she would do the laundry and cooking for the wagon train. The caravan consisted of about thirty wagons carrying five families and twenty-six single men. Since the group had so few women, having a cook and laundress on the trip would help a lot. Wadsworth gladly agreed to Clara's proposal.

The wagons were sturdily built, designed to provide low resistance to high winds, with covers of heavy white canvas. Each wagon was pulled by a team of six oxen. A typical wagon carried a load of two or three tons. Among the supplies needed for the long overland journey were such items as soap, matches, tools, cooking equipment, and wood-burning field stoves. The foodstuffs included bacon, dried beans, rice, flour, sugar, salt, coffee, tea, dried apples, and plenty of water kegs. They also carried rifles, not only to hunt rabbits, prairie chickens, buffalo, and other game to supplement their food supplies, but also for self-defense against large wild animals and Indian raiders.

At the time she left Kansas, Clara was about fifty-nine or sixty years old. Because she was black, those in charge of the wagon train felt that it was not proper for her to ride in the wagons with the other women. So Clara had to walk the six hundred miles to Denver behind the wagon train.

The trip was a challenging experience for Clara. When the wagons stopped at noon, Clara prepared lunch and cleaned up afterward. The caravan stopped again in the late afternoon and set up camp for the night. The travelers arranged the wagons in a protective circle and built a few fires in the center. While the others tended to their own chores, Clara milked the cows, washed the laundry, baked bread in a Dutch oven, made butter, and cooked the evening meal over a campfire. At bedtime she slept wrapped in a blanket under one of the wagons. In the morning, Clara was up early to prepare breakfast and clean up quickly before the caravan was off again. This pattern of life on the trail was repeated day after day for two months. On Sundays, the wagon train rested, giving Clara some time to read her Bible.

There were good travel days, and bad days when they moved slowly, toiling through bad weather or difficult terrain. Sometimes the travelers met up with wagons carrying discouraged people who had given up and turned back due to excessive hardships. Between Smoky Hill and the Republican River was a particularly difficult stretch, where there were no water sources to replenish the train's supplies. Here, Clara's caravan went for several days without water. Some members of the party kept a slice of dried apple under their tongue to keep their mouths moist; a few even sucked on a bullet for the same purpose.

On June 8, 1859, the wagon train reached its destination, the small mining town of Cherry Creek, near today's Denver. By chance, Clara stopped to eat in a small restaurant and bakery run by a German family. Learning that Clara had served in a German home and knew German cooking, they put her right to work while she was getting settled in town.

Upon her arrival in Cherry Creek, Clara immediately looked for a church to join. She met a small group of Methodists who did not yet have a church building or a pastor, but they were expecting a minister, Jacob Adriance, to arrive soon. Clara's Methodist friends also advised her about the local situation. They told her that some of the gold seekers who came into town soon left to look for better claims, leaving their cabins empty. Some of these homes could be purchased for as little as twenty-five dollars. Clara bought one of these cabins and promptly set up her laundry business, placing a sign in front of her house. Some of her first customers were those she had met on the wagon train. It was not long before Clara had a thriving little business. In the meantime, she continued to ask everyone she met if they had ever seen or heard of her daughter, Eliza Jane. No one had.

When the minister arrived, Clara eagerly attended his prayer meetings. She also brought him soup and pies and helped him organize the congregation, raise money for a church, and even establish a Sunday school. In addition, Clara often made food for the needy in Cherry Creek, cared for the sick, and generally devoted herself to Christian charity and kindness. At Christmastime, it was Clara who prepared the turkey dinner for everyone who came to Reverend Adriance's cabin for the Yuletide celebration.

After a few months, Reverend Adriance decided not to build his church in Cherry Creek but rather to go to Central City, whose larger population, he felt, had a more urgent need for his church. When he left in 1860, Clara decided to go, too. She could afford the stagecoach ticket to Central City, but black people were not allowed to travel independently, so she paid a white man to accompany her, posing as his slave.

Central City was a wild town, where drinking, gambling, and fist-fights were common. Nevertheless, Clara made herself at home. She bought a two-room cabin and opened the first laundry in Central City. Friendly and hardworking, she soon became a beloved figure. The townspeople called her Aunt Clara Brown, "Aunt" being a title of respect. She continued her charity work, feeding the hungry, tending the sick, and even delivering babies. Sometimes she took in ailing miners and cared for them until they could go back to work. Some of these grateful prospectors gave Aunt Clara papers assigning her a share of their profits.

Clara began investing her money in houses in Central City, Georgetown, Denver, Idaho Springs, and Boulder, as well as in some mines in the area. Within ten years, she had accumulated $10,000, an amazing amount of money for that time. Throughout her years in Central City, she continued to inquire constantly about her lost daughter.

In 1864 Clara lost some of her investments when a flood swept through Denver and destroyed most of the town. It not only washed away the houses she owned there, but also papers that proved her ownership of some of her properties. Clara was not financially ruined, however, as she still had other properties, some savings, and income from her business.

In 1866, after the Civil War had ended, Clara purchased a stage-coach ticket back to Kentucky, where she hoped to find relatives, old friends, and word of Eliza Jane. She later continued her search in

Tennessee. There she found a number of former slaves in desperate straits. She gathered some men and women together and organized a wagon train to take them to Colorado, paying the costs herself.

The arrival of this large group of former slaves in Colorado was noted in the *Rocky Mountain News*, which called Clara Brown "a woman in a thousand." Before the group's arrival, there were only twenty-three African Americans in Denver, but Clara's party doubled that number. In Denver, Clara helped her companions find homes and employment. These and other benevolent actions earned her the nickname "Angel of the Rockies."

Back in Central City, Clara continued to be active in the church. She often used her own house to hold church services and Sunday school before the building of St. James Methodist Church, which she helped establish. St. James was dedicated on July 21, 1872. Clara also gave money to support four other churches in Central City, including the First Presbyterian Church, which she sometimes attended.

In 1873 another disaster struck that weakened Clara's financial stability. A fire in Central City burned several of the houses that Clara owned there, further reducing her already depleted assets. She moved into a cottage that belonged to a friend, operating her laundry business from there for several years.

In 1879, after Reconstruction ended, many former slaves moved to Kansas in what was sometimes called the Black Exodus. Colorado governor Frederick Pitkin enlisted Clara Brown to travel by train to Kansas as an official representative of the state, asking her to encourage these black settlers, known as Exodusters, to consider moving to Colorado. Most of the Exodusters were very poor, and Clara took along money donated by a number of Colorado churches to help them. She also contributed some of her own remaining money to this effort. Clara remained in Kansas for a year, all the while still looking for information about her daughter. Then, in failing health at age seventy-nine, she returned to Central City.

By this time Clara was having serious money problems. After losing so many of her investments in flood and in fire, and having given away a substantial amount of money to churches and to help newly freed slaves, she was almost penniless. But the people of Colorado did not abandon her. An anonymous donor gave her a small house in Denver, and friends provided her with food, clothing, and personal care.

It was February 14, 1882, when Clara received a letter from an old friend from Denver who now lived in Iowa. The woman wrote that she thought she might have found Eliza Jane. She had met a middle-aged widow named Eliza Jane in Council Bluffs, Iowa. This Eliza Jane said she was originally from Kentucky and had had a twin sister who drowned in the Big Muddy River. Clara knew in her heart that it was indeed her Eliza Jane. After forty-six years of searching, Clara had finally found her daughter.

Clara did not have the money to travel to Iowa, but her Colorado friends stepped in to help. An article appeared in the *Denver Republican* explaining Clara's situation and asking for donations. The Union Pacific Railroad agreed to help by offering to sell Clara a round-trip ticket at half price. All the arrangements were quickly made, and Clara wrote to her Iowa friend asking her to arrange a meeting with her daughter in Council Bluffs on Saturday, March 4. Friends sent Clara off at the train station with some money and a basket of food, and she was soon on her way to see her beloved Eliza Jane.

During the joyous reunion, Clara met Eliza Jane's grown daughter, Cindy. After a long visit in Iowa, Clara's daughter and grand-daughter returned with her to Denver to live. At long last, Clara had her own family.

In the early 1880s, volunteers petitioned the Society of Colorado Pioneers to include Clara in their membership. The society, established by the state of Colorado in 1872, was open to white men who settled in Colorado prior to 1860, and those granted this designation received a small pension from the state. In the beginning, no African Americans were included in the group, and women could be only honorary members. But the petitioners argued that Clara Brown, who certainly qualified as one of the state's early settlers, deserved to be included. Their effort succeeded, and in 1885, the last year of her life, Clara Brown became the first black member as well as the first female member of the organization. Just one month before her death, on September 24, 1885, the Society of Colorado Pioneers honored Clara at a special banquet. She sat at the table in a wheelchair, with her daughter sitting on one side and her granddaughter on the other.

Aunt Clara Brown died peacefully in her sleep on October 26, 1885. She was buried in Denver's Riverside Cemetery. A huge crowd attended her funeral. Among the mourners were the mayor of Denver and the governor of Colorado. A memorial article in the *Denver Tribune Republic* said, "We hold in grateful remembrance the kind old friend . . . who rising from the humble position of a slave to the angelic type of noble woman, won our sympathy and commanded our respect."

Over the years, many tributes have been made to the memory of Clara Brown. A bronze plaque at St. James Methodist Church explains that their first services in Central City were held at Clara's home. In 1930 a memorial chair in her name was installed at the Central City Opera House. In 1977 a stained glass portrait of Clara was installed in the rotunda of the Colorado State Capitol, alongside other great figures in Colorado history. And an opera about Clara's life, *Gabriel's Daughter*, debuted in the Central City Opera House in 2003.

Clara Brown is remembered as one of Colorado's great pioneers. Her concern extended to all those in need, regardless of color or religious affiliation. She truly was the Angel of the Rockies.

Isabella Bird Bishop, circa mid-1890s —Courtesy
Western History Collection, Denver Public Library

2

ISABELLA BIRD

"From the Summit"

In the autumn of 1873, world traveler Isabella Bird, returning from a long visit in Hawaii, decided to stop off in Colorado before sailing home to Scotland. While passing through the Rocky Mountains, she dreamed about climbing the famous Longs Peak—sometimes called America's Matterhorn—near Estes Park.

A few weeks later, Isabella and two guides on horseback passed near the entrance to Estes Park, where they spied a small, crude log cabin with smoke coming out the chimney. A dog in front of the cabin began growling, which brought the owner outside. The man, a frontiersman known as Rocky Mountain Jim, made quite an impression on Isabella. In a letter to her sister, she described the meeting: He wore "a grey hunting suit, much the worse for wear (almost falling to pieces, in fact), a knife in his belt . . . [and] a revolver sticking out of the breast pocket of his coat; his feet . . . were bare except for some dilapidated moccasins made of horse hide. His face was remarkable. He is a man about forty-five, and must have been strikingly handsome. . . . Tawny hair, in thin, uncared-for curls fell from under his hunter's cap and over his collar. One eye was entirely gone, and the loss made one side of his face repulsive, while the other might have been modeled in marble. 'Desperado' was written in large letters all over him."

Little did Isabella know, at that moment, that this "desperado" would soon be her guide on a treacherous climb up Longs Peak.

Isabella Bird was only a visitor to Colorado, but her adventures through the Rocky Mountains earned her a place in the state's history. Her daring travels in the Estes Park area, including climbing Long's Peak with Rocky Mountain Jim, were the heart of her famous book *A Lady's Life in the Rocky Mountains*.

Isabella Lucy Bird was born on October 10, 1831, in Boroughbridge Parish in the English county of North Yorkshire. Her father, Edward Bird, was an Anglican clergyman, and her mother, Dora Lawson Bird, was the daughter of a clergyman and taught Sunday school. Isabella did have female adventurers in her bloodline, though: two of her aunts were missionaries, one in India and another in Persia (today's Iran).

Isabella was educated at home by her parents. Her father taught her Latin and botany, while her mother instructed her in literature, history, drawing, French, and of course, the Bible. Young Isabella made use of her father's large library, and she read the entire Bible while still a child. Both Isabella and her younger sister, Henrietta (Hennie), received strong religious training from their parents.

The family moved a number of times as Edward Bird changed parishes, but they always spent part of every summer in Scotland. Edward loved not only Scotland's natural beauty but also the fact that the Scottish people shared his strong belief that no work should be done on Sundays, a commandment that many of his English parishioners ignored.

Isabella was a small and sickly child. She often complained of back pain, headaches, insomnia, depression, and other ailments, though her health always improved in the Scottish Highlands. When she was eighteen, she had an operation to remove a tumor from her spine. Although the operation was successful, Isabella's overall health did not improve. Her doctor suggested that a sea voyage might help her recover, so Isabella made several short trips to the Outer Hebrides Islands. She wrote a number of articles about her travels there, which were published anonymously in several family magazines including *The Family Treasury* and *The Sunday Magazine*.

When Isabella was twenty-three, her father gave her £100 to travel wherever she liked. She sailed to North America in 1854, spending seven months in Nova Scotia, Prince Edward Island, Ontario, Chicago, Boston, and New York. She said that the trip dispelled many of the prejudices she had about Americans—many Europeans believed Americans to be loud, rude, and uneducated, but Isabella found them friendly and well informed. Moreover, Isabella found that her health indeed improved while abroad.

While she was away, she wrote long letters to her sister Henrietta. When she came home to England, she used the contents of the letters to write a book, *The English Woman in America*, which was published in 1856. Years before, in the Hebrides Islands, Isabella had become interested in the difficult conditions of the crofters (tenant farmers), who eked out a tenuous living there. After the publication of her book, she used some of the royalties to help a number of Scottish crofters who had immigrated to America. On later trips to the States, Isabella checked up on the welfare of these crofters and was pleased to see that they were doing well in their adopted country.

After her father died in 1858, Isabella, her sister, and her mother moved to Edinburgh, Scotland, which would be her home for the rest of her life. Now twenty-nine, Isabella was again in poor health, as she usually was when she was home. For a while, she spent her days resting in bed until noon, often writing, and then getting up and doing volunteer work, such as serving on various church committees, in the afternoon. After their mother died in 1866, the two sisters continued to live in Edinburgh, where Isabella stayed until her doctor recommended she try another overseas trip. She did not need much persuasion.

Over the next few years, Isabella made three trips to North America and one to the Mediterranean. She took with her a fairly new invention—a camera, which she learned to use proficiently. Isabella took many photographs during her travels, developing the film herself, and created some striking images to accompany her writing. As she became a seasoned traveler, she often stayed in local inns or, when weather permitted, camped out. She was not fussy about what she ate, and one of her relatives remarked that she had the appetite of a tiger and the ironlike digestion of an ostrich.

In 1872, at age forty, Isabella set off on a longer journey, sailing to Australia and New Zealand. After two months in these places, she found she disliked the climate and decided to leave. Instead of going home, however, she sailed across the Pacific to Hawaii. She loved the Hawaiian Islands (often called the Sandwich Islands in those days) and stayed for six months.

During her time in Hawaii, Isabella learned to ride astride a horse, which she found much easier on her back than riding sidesaddle. In those days, riding astride was considered improper for a lady, as was wearing pants. Like a few other bold women of the era, Isabella defied these Victorian restrictions and chose to wear bloomers, a type of baggy pants worn underneath a shortened skirt. She referred to them as "Turkish trousers."

Isabella adored the outdoor life of Hawaii, writing, "This is the height of enjoyment in traveling. I have just encamped under a lauhala tree, with my saddle inverted for a pillow, my horse tied by a long lariat to a guava bush." She traveled by mule to Mauna Loa, the highest volcano in the islands, which was active at the time and emitted impressive smoke and sparks. The intrepid Isabella climbed to the top of the volcano and camped near its rim.

From Hawaii, Isabella journeyed to the American West Coast, visiting San Francisco then taking a train to Truckee, California, where she hired a horse and went off exploring. She came upon the stunning Lake Tahoe and spent the night at an inn there. In an essay about Lake Tahoe, she wrote, "I have found a dream of beauty at which one might look all one's life and sigh." Isabella herself, however, was not one to sit and sigh in one spot all her life, no matter how beautiful. She rode back to Truckee and took the night train to Greeley, Colorado, where she began her famous journey into the Rocky Mountains.

When Isabella stepped off the train in Greeley in early September 1873, Colorado was still a territory, and she found herself in a wide-open world of prairie dogs and pioneer wagons. Her eyes were not fixed on the prairies, however, but on Longs Peak, rising high into the blue autumn skies. Isabella made it her goal to get to Estes Park and climb this mountain. She would not be the first woman to do so—only a few weeks earlier, Anna Dickinson, an American writer, had claimed the title of the first female ever to scale Longs Peak.

Isabella took a buggy into the foothills and stayed briefly in the cabin of some settlers. The settlers, a couple named Chalmer, agreed to guide her to Estes Park, but they turned out to be very poor guides. In fact, after wandering about lost, cold, bruised, and hungry for several days, they were lucky to find their way back to the cabin again.

In late September, Isabella made her way to Longmont. With winter approaching, she feared she would have to return to Scotland without realizing her goal of climbing Longs Peak. Luckily, the innkeeper in Longmont arranged for Isabella to ride along with two young men who had stopped at the hotel and were leaving in the morning on horseback for Estes Park.

On reaching the entrance to Estes Park at Muggin's Gulch, the party of three met James Nugent, known throughout the area as Rocky Mountain Jim. It was a brief encounter, but the man, with his bizarre appearance that belied his almost courtly behavior, made quite an impression on her.

Isabella and her two companions rode on into Estes Park, where she rented a comfortable cabin from a local settler named Griffith (Griff) Evans. When she mentioned her ambition to her host, he told her it was too late in the year to risk climbing Longs Peak, which was a difficult ascent even in good weather. But when Evans left for business in Denver a few days later, Jim Nugent, the strange man she'd met on the day of her arrival in the area, appeared at the Evans ranch and offered to guide Isabella up the 14,700-foot peak. She and Jim, along with the two young men who had accompanied her to Estes Park, decided to make the climb immediately.

The next day, after gathering a few supplies, they rode up the trail past Lily Lake to camp. Along the way, Jim rode up alongside Isabella and began to chat. "With a grace of manner which soon made me forget his appearance, [we] entered into a conversation which lasted for more than three hours, in spite of the manifold checks of fording streams, single file, abrupt ascents and descents, and other incidents of mountain travel." That night, the temperature fell below freezing. An excited Isabella found it hard to sleep.

The next morning, after observing an exquisite sunrise, the climbers tethered the horses and left the supplies in camp to begin the difficult ascent on foot. Rocky Mountain Jim tied Isabella to him by a rope and essentially hauled her up the mountain. At times, Isabella crawled on her hands and knees. A few times she slipped and swung in the air by the rope until Jim hoisted her up. In a letter to her sister, she wrote, "You know I have no head and no ankles, and never ought to dream of mountaineering; and had I known that the ascent was a real mountaineer feat, I should not have felt the slightest ambition to perform it. As it is, I am only humiliated at my success for Jim dragged me up like a bale of goods."

After a long and treacherous climb, they miraculously reached the top. Though bruised, exhausted, and gasping for breath in the high altitude, Isabella was deeply moved:

From the summit were seen in unrivalled combination all the views which had rejoiced our eyes during the ascent. It was something at last to stand upon the storm-rent crown of this lonely sentinel of the Rocky Range, on one of the mightiest of the vertebrae of the backbone of the North American continent, and to see the waters start for both oceans. Uplifted above love and hate and storms of passion, calm amidst the eternal silences, fanned by zephyrs and bathed in living blue, peace rested for that one bright day on the Peak.

They did not stay long, however; the climbers were weak with thirst and it was growing late. The two young men decided to go down by themselves, while Jim sought out the easiest possible route for Isabella. Jim went down first, with Isabella's feet on his shoulders. She frequently slipped on the icy rock but suffered no serious falls. At one point, Isabella's skirt caught on a rock, leaving her dangling until Jim cut her loose with his hunting knife.

All four made it safely back to camp, whereupon the cold, battered, and exhausted Isabella immediately crawled off to sleep. She awoke after a few hours to warm up by the campfire, where she sat until morning with Jim, looking at the stars and listening with rapt attention to his colorful tales.

Upon returning to Griff Evans's ranch in Estes Park, Isabella decided to stay on as a guest for a few more weeks. She wrote, "I really need nothing more than this log cabin offers." Some days she went out with Griff Evans and his men to drive cattle. In the evenings, they sang songs and spun stories. Then of course, there was the main attraction: frequent visits from Jim Nugent. As the unlikely friendship between Isabella and Rocky Mountain Jim blossomed, they became the talk of the settlement. Griff Evans in particular became more and more irritated about their growing relationship. Isabella realized the two men were not friends but rivals, both as guides and as local celebrities in Estes Park.

MY HOME IN THE ROCKY MOUNTAINS

Sketch of Isabella Bird's cabin in Colorado —From *A Lady's Life in the Rocky Mountains*, published in 1879

After a few weeks, and perhaps to escape from the attraction she felt for Jim Nugent, Isabella left Estes Park determined to see more of Colorado on her own. She rode into Longmont, accompanied by a young Canadian man she'd met at Griff's ranch and mounted upon her new horse, Birdie. From Longmont she proceeded to Denver, where she visited with *Rocky Mountain News* editor William N. Byers and former territorial governor A. Cameron Hunt. She then set off from Denver alone on horseback to explore the Colorado Territory, following a circular route.

It was an exhilarating but dangerous trip, much of it through snow, ice, and bitter cold. At times she had to dismount and walk because Birdie's hooves had become encrusted with ice. Although she passed through much wilderness, Isabella managed to find shelter each night at various settlers' cabins. She traveled this way, riding ten hours a day, for almost three weeks. She praised the fortitude of Birdie, calling her "the queen of the ponies." Isabella traveled over five hundred miles, visiting South Park, the Garden of the Gods, the Continental Divide, Green Lake, and other wondrous places before returning to Denver. Isabella did not stay long in Denver, which was "full of rowdies," before going back to Estes Park.

It was now mid-November, and Estes Park was quieter with the advent of winter; Griff Evans was out of town, and no visitors remained at the ranch. But Jim Nugent was still there, and the attraction between the two of them was evident. Isabella observed that Jim had become very moody. A few days later, Jim invited her to ride with him to check his beaver traps. While out on the snowy trail, he told her the sad story of his life, "how a man can become a devil," as he put it. Isabella was both thrilled and appalled by Jim's frank disclosures. He admitted how fond he was of her, but felt that she had "stirred the better nature in me too late," concluding, "You won't speak to me again, will you?" Yet the next time he saw her, he made no reference to their previous conversation. Isabella, though perplexed and sad, managed to remain friends with Rocky Mountain Jim for the remainder of her stay in Colorado. In a letter to her sister, she wrote, "He is a man whom any woman might love, but whom no sane woman would marry. Nor," she added, "did he ask me to marry him."

In early December, Isabella decided to leave Colorado before she was snowed in until spring. She bid goodbye to her friends in Estes Park and to her faithful mare, Birdie. Jim rode with her nearly fifty miles to Loveland (then called St. Louis), where she would catch a stagecoach to Cheyenne, and from there, a train to New York. Although the two would exchange letters, the lady and the mountain man never saw each other again. One day she received the terrible news that Jim had been shot and killed by Griff Evans.

From New York, Isabella boarded a ship to England and made her way back to her sister in Scotland. There she worked on her new book, based on her trip to Hawaii. *Six Months in the Sandwich Islands* was published in 1875. She later chronicled her adventures in Colorado in the book *A Lady's Life in the Rocky Mountains*, published in 1879.

In the meantime, in 1878, Isabella set off for her next destination: the Far East. Her first stop was Japan. Never content just to see the well-known tourist areas, she traveled through the primitive countryside with a young Japanese guide and interpreter she'd hired in San Francisco. She ventured to Hokkaido, in the far north of Japan, where she lived for a time with the Ainu tribe, the original inhabitants of the island of Japan. After Japan Isabella explored Hong Kong, Canton, Saigon, and Singapore. From there she went to the Malay Peninsula, where she stayed for five weeks. During her travels, she used all forms of transportation. In Malaysia she rode an elephant, and in the mountainous Tibetan regions of China she rode a yak. She always returned home to her sister for a time, only to become restless again.

In 1879 Isabella's sister fell ill with typhoid, and Isabella hurried back to Scotland to be with her. Tending Henrietta during her illness was Dr. John Bishop, a longtime family friend. John had asked Isabella to marry him in 1877, but at that time, she did not want to settle down with a husband. Less than a year after Isabella returned home, in spite of having the best of care, Henrietta died. The following spring, Isabella married the good Dr. Bishop. While the two lived happily married in Scotland, Isabella published three more books, all based on her trip to Asia. Not long after they were married, however, John fell ill from "blood poisoning" (pernicious anemia), and he was sick on and off for the next several years. Then in 1886, only five years after their marriage, John died.

After the death of her husband, Isabella tried to keep busy with nursing and helping the poor in Scotland and giving drawing lessons to local students. Before long, however, her lifelong wanderlust came over her again. In 1889 she went to India as a medical missionary. While there she established the Henrietta Bird Hospital in Amritsar and the John Bishop Memorial Hospital in Srinagar. Isabella traveled on horseback to Kashmir and Ladakh, near the Tibetan border. During this trip, her horse lost its footing and fell into a river. The horse drowned, but Isabella survived the accident with two broken ribs.

In January 1890 in Shimla, India, Isabella met Maj. Herbert Sawyer, a British officer on his way to a new assignment in Persia (today's Iran). Isabella joined the major's small party as they traveled in mid-winter through the desert, arriving in Teheran much the worse for wear. While in the Middle East, Isabella had to wear a long hooded robe and a veil, as it was forbidden for women to be seen uncovered (and in many places it still is). Shortly after arriving in Teheran, Isabella left the major at his post and continued on by herself through northern Iran. Later she hired a small caravan and traveled through Kurdistan to the Black Sea, where she took a steamer to Constantinople (Istanbul), Turkey. During her trip through these countries, she witnessed atrocities committed against Christian Armenians and vowed to make the situation known to the Western world.

Arriving back in Great Britain in late December 1890, Isabella found she had made a name for herself from her travel books. She used her new celebrity to gain an interview with British Prime Minister William Gladstone, determined to tell him about the persecutions of Christians she had seen in Kurdistan and Turkey. She later testified before a Parliamentary committee about the abuses she had observed. Her fame as a world traveler also earned her a special honor—in 1891 she became the first woman to be inducted into the

Royal Geographical Society. She was later elected to membership in the Royal Photographic Society as well.

Isabella's next two books recollected her travels in the Middle East and central Asia. *Journeys to Persia and Kurdistan* was published in 1891, and *Among the Tibetans* came out in 1893. Although she was now in her sixties, Isabella's adventures were far from over. In 1894, at age sixty-three, she set out on a three-year-trip to the Far East. She went first to Yokohama, Japan, and from there to Korea, where she spent several months. After Korea, she went to China and traveled up the Yangtze River as far as she could go in a sampan (skiff). She then went overland to Sichuan, where she found herself in considerable danger. A large mob, calling her a "foreign devil," attacked the hotel she was in and set it on fire. She barely escaped with her life, rescued by a detachment of local soldiers. Soon after, at another place, villagers threw stones at her, knocking her unconscious. Still, she did not turn back.

In 1897 Isabella returned to England and recorded her most recent adventures in a series of books, including *Korea and Her Neighbours* (1898) and *The Yangtze Valley and Beyond* (1899). Throughout her travels, Isabella had taken many photographs and developed the film herself, creating some striking images. Most of her previous works were illustrated with her photos, and she published some books of photography as well, including *Views in the Far East*, published in 1897, and *Pictures From China* (also published as *Chinese Pictures*), published in 1900.

In 1901, at age seventy, Isabella embarked on her final trip, this time to Morocco, where she spent three years. After returning home, while planning yet another trip to China, she fell ill. Her health declined rapidly due to heart disease and a large fibroid tumor. Her last days were spent in in Edinburgh, where she died on October 7, 1904, just a few days before her seventy-third birthday.

Many decades later, British playwright Caryl Churchill featured Isabella Bird as a character in her 1982 feminist play, *Top Girls*. Isabella was indeed at the very top of female adventurers. Although she'd traveled all over the globe, she especially cherished her time in Colorado and her romantic adventure climbing Longs Peak with Rocky Mountain Jim. "I would not," she wrote, "exchange my memories of the perfect beauty and extraordinary sublimity for any other experience of mountaineering in any part of the world."

Augusta Pierce Tabor, circa 1880s —Courtesy Western
History Collection, Denver Public Library

3
AUGUSTA TABOR

First Lady of Leadville

Looking back on her pioneering life in Colorado, Augusta Tabor wrote, "I feel that in those early years of self-sacrifice, hard labor, and economy, I laid the foundation for Mr. Tabor's immense wealth. Had I not stayed with him and worked by his side, he would have been discouraged, returned to the stone-cutting trade."

Supported by his wife, Horace (Haw) Tabor was in the right place at the right time. In 1878 in Leadville, Colorado, Haw's dream of mining success came true. He had spent years prospecting for gold and silver with little to show for it, but he continued to grubstake other miners, giving them food and supplies in exchange for a promise of a share of the wealth if they found rich ore. Unfortunately, time after time, they found as little as he had. Then came his lucky day. Two German miners he had grubstaked struck it rich, making Haw Tabor rich, too. He could now buy his wife, Augusta, anything she wanted.

But Augusta wanted little. She was content with what she already had, running their store in the small mining town where her husband was mayor and being recognized as the "first lady of Leadville." After twenty years of hard work, Augusta could finally enjoy a simple but secure life, and she was happy. But now that her husband, who had failed so often at prospecting, was Leadville's "Silver King," Augusta's life was about to change.

Born in Augusta, Maine, on March 29, 1833, Augusta Louise Pierce was one of seven daughters and three sons in the family of William B. Pierce and Lucy Eaton Pierce. Augusta was a sickly child, but she survived, it was said, through sheer willpower. Named for the capital city of her native state, Augusta lived a life of comfort in a lovely New England home where the family was wealthy enough to have servants. Her father, the well-respected owner of a stone-cutting business, owned more than one hundred acres of land in Augusta. William Pierce was also related to future U.S. president Franklin Pierce.

In August 1854, when Augusta was twenty-one, Horace Austin Warner (Haw) Tabor, age twenty-three, came to work for William Pierce, and he boarded in the Pierce household. This brought Augusta in close contact with Haw, and before long, the two fell in love and became engaged.

Haw thought the couple's best opportunity for a bright future was in the West, and he told Augusta that he wanted go to Kansas, establish a farm, and come back to marry her. Persuading Augusta to go along with his plan, Haw left for Kansas Territory, where he homesteaded a 160-acre farm on Deep Creek in Riley County. As promised, he came back to Maine and married Augusta on January 31, 1857, in the living room of the Pierce family home. Augusta's father gave the couple $300 as a wedding gift—$200 to Augusta and $100 to Haw. A few weeks later, on February 25, Augusta left for Kansas with her new husband.

The couple took a train to St. Louis, then boarded a steamboat to Kansas City, where they bought a pair of oxen, a cart, farm implements, and general supplies. They set off for their homestead accompanied by two friends, Samuel Kellogg and Nathaniel Maxcy, who would be helping the Tabors with their farm. The men walked the 120-mile distance while Augusta rode in the cart. The party arrived in Manhattan, Kansas, on April 19, 1857.

When the Tabors reached their homestead, they found a surprise waiting for them. While Haw was back in Maine, some of his new Kansas friends had pitched in and built the newlyweds a house. It was a simple log cabin that contained little but a stove. While it was a lovely gesture, Augusta was not prepared for the primitive conditions of the western prairie. She wrote:

> I shall never forget the morning of my arrival. To add to the desolation of the place, one of the Kansas winds was blowing, furiously. Sitting upon an open prairie, one half mile from any cabin, was my future home—a log cabin, 12 by 16 feet; not an outhouse, or a stone, or stick in sight. . . . I sat down upon an old trunk, the only thing to sit on, and the tears began to flow copiously. . . . After a few hours I dried my tears, cleaned up the cabin, and prepared the first meal.

She served that meal, salt pork and beans, on a white linen tablecloth with sterling silver cutlery unpacked from her bridal gifts.

Nothing in Augusta's privileged upbringing had prepared her to be a pioneer farmer, but with energy and determination, she became one. She sowed seeds and cared for the crops, cooked the meals, and tended to the household chores. Grasshoppers ate most of their crop the first year, but the Tabors and their two helpers persevered. That October, Haw and Augusta became the parents of a son, Maxcy, named after their friend Nathaniel Maxcy. The Tabors tried farming for another year, but a drought coupled with poor markets made it very difficult to continue.

Things were looking very dismal for the Tabors when Haw heard about gold strikes in the region known as Colorado, in western Kansas Territory. He and Augusta decided to give up on farming and go prospecting for gold. On April 5, 1859, the Tabor family, along with Nathaniel Maxcy and Samuel Kellogg, set out for the goldfields in an ox-drawn wagon, taking a load of supplies and a small number of cattle. They reached the outskirts of what is now Denver on June 20 and camped there for two weeks before moving on to the main mining camp in Golden.

The men set up a tent in Golden to serve as a house for Augusta and little Maxcy, then they set out on foot for Gregory Diggings (now called Central City). Augusta, on her own with the baby and the cattle, waited for the return of the men. They finally came back, after a few weeks, without having found anything of value. Discouraged, they loaded the wagon and set out for the mountains, where they hoped to find better claims.

Three weeks later, the Tabors and their two companions reached what is now Idaho Springs, Colorado. In her journal Augusta wrote, "I was the first white woman there, if white I could be called, after camping out three months." This time the men built a log house for Augusta and Maxcy, putting the tent on top for a roof. For the time being, at least, Augusta was settled.

After the men went out prospecting again, Augusta opened her first business, selling milk and home-cooked food to the miners in the camp. Although Haw found no gold, Augusta made enough money to finish paying for their farm in Kansas with some left over, allowing the family to spend the winter more comfortably in the larger town of Denver. Haw made several more prospecting trips but continued to come up empty-handed.

Determined to find a good lode, Haw moved his family two more times, finally settling at California Gulch, where Augusta again found herself the first white woman in camp, in May 1860. At this camp, the men built her a log cabin with a sod roof and a dirt floor, and when Haw went off prospecting, Augusta again set up shop to earn money serving the miners. This time, in addition to selling meals and baked goods, she took in boarders and, using a scale she had brought with her, weighed prospectors' gold dust for a fee. As more gold seekers moved into the camp, the place took the name of Oro City, and soon a post office was needed. Augusta was happy to be appointed postmistress, adding it to her string of responsibilities.

Finally Haw had some success, too. By September of that year, he had accumulated $5,000 in gold dust from his mining claim. He gave Augusta $1,000 to spend as she wished. First she bought another 160 acres of land in Kansas, adjacent to their original farm, then, eager for her parents to meet their grandson, she used most of the rest of the money to take Haw and Maxcy back to Maine for a long visit. When it was time to return to Colorado, the Tabors took a train to St. Joseph, Missouri, where they bought a pair of mules and a wagon. On their way home, they spent the money they had left to buy flour.

After arriving back in Oro City in the spring of 1861, the Tabors reopened the store in their cabin. As before, Augusta ran the store while Haw continued working his mining claim. That summer, the store proved more profitable than the claim. Augusta also made extra money by occasionally transporting gold for the postal express, riding a horse back and forth to Denver.

When the placer gold in Oro City began to run out several months later, people started leaving the area, so the Tabors followed suit. This time they went to a camp called Buckskin Joe. Haw had no better luck mining there, so he finally quit prospecting and helped Augusta set up another store and post office. Although he was no longer mining himself, Haw, who always believed a big strike was just around the corner, continued to grubstake other miners, giving them supplies from the store in return for a share of any riches they discovered. Augusta, however, disapproved of the grubstaking, feeling that her husband was throwing away good money.

In 1868, when mining activity in Buckskin Joe dried up, the Tabors moved back to Oro City, where some new mines had opened. They established a new store and settled into what was by now their normal routine. When silver was discovered a mile away, prospectors began pouring into the area and the Tabors moved closer to the new camp, where they built another store with combined living quarters. The bedrooms were upstairs, while the kitchen and dining room were in the rear of the store. The Tabors' new store did a lively business, and soon they had to hire two clerks to help them. They also opened what was essentially a bank, using the big store safe to hold the miners' cash.

In January 1878, enough people lived in the camp that the residents held a meeting to charter a town. They chose the name Leadville and elected Haw Tabor as their first mayor. The Tabors' success continued, and before long, they built a roomy new house,

Tabor house in Leadville
—Courtesy Western History Collection, Denver Public Library

leaving the rooms above the store for their clerks to live in. At her new home, Augusta was still busy, running what amounted to a restaurant, serving meals to miners. Meanwhile, Haw continued to grubstake prospectors.

In April 1878, Haw gave $17 worth of supplies to two German miners, August Rische and George Hook. A few days later, he gave the pair another $50 worth of goods. In exchange, the miners signed Haw's usual agreement, promising him one-third of whatever they found.

Lo and behold, a short time later, the two Germans struck it rich. Their mine, the Little Pittsburg, would bring Haw $500,000 over the next fifteen months. Haw immediately invested in another mine, the Chrysolite, which was also very successful. All that summer, paying little attention to their newly acquired wealth, Augusta continued to live modestly and to work in the store and restaurant. But by the fall, Haw was not only rich, he had been elected lieutenant governor of Colorado, so the family would have to move to Denver, the state capital. Augusta's life as the "first lady of Leadville" was at an end.

Moving to Denver in January 1879, the Tabors bought the luxurious former home of Henry C. Brown. By this time Denver was a modern, cultivated city. While Augusta settled in at the Denver house, Haw, eager to go out and enjoy his wealth and prestige, started spending many of his evenings out on the town. He visited saloons, dance halls, and bordellos and began numerous affairs, which Augusta soon discovered. Although she was upset, Haw promised to end his philandering, and Augusta stayed with him.

In September 1879 Haw sold his interest in the Little Pittsburg Mine for $1 million. He then bought another mine, the Matchless Mine, which proved to have the richest silver deposits in Leadville. He also purchased stock in the First National Bank of Denver and made various other investments. With his new fortune, Haw began construction on the Tabor Opera House in Leadville, moving there to oversee the project while Augusta remained in Denver. He lived in an apartment on the second floor of the opera house, which had a passageway leading to the Clarendon Hotel next door. Haw remained in Leadville for months, not even coming home for Christmas. Even after Haw returned to Denver, the Tabor marriage remained deeply troubled.

In the spring of 1880, Haw, now forty-nine, met a spirited, twenty-five-year-old beauty named Elizabeth McCourt Doe, known by all as "Baby" Doe. Baby had recently divorced her husband, Harvey Doe, a failed miner and ne'er-do-well. Haw was instantly captivated by her charm, and Baby Doe returned his interest. By early autumn, the situation had reached the point that Haw and Augusta separated, and Haw moved into a suite of rooms at the Windsor Hotel, of which he was part owner, in Denver. As Haw's affair with Baby Doe grew more serious, he finally asked Augusta, in January 1881, for a divorce. In spite of a handsome settlement offer, Augusta refused.

Not only did Augusta deny Haw the divorce, she raised the stakes by buying a one-third interest in the Windsor Hotel, where Haw was living. She now co-owned the hotel with Haw and Bill Bush, who managed the place; Maxcy Tabor was Bush's assistant manager. The hotel was a good investment—as with all her properties, the Windsor earned Augusta a nice profit—but it was also a way for Augusta to keep a closer eye on her husband. Both Haw and Bill Bush tried to buy out her share, but she would not sell.

In the late summer of 1881, after a lengthy trip abroad, Augusta learned that her husband had finished building a new opera house in Denver. Constructed at an estimated cost of $800,000, the Tabor Grand Opera House was reputed to be one of the finest theaters in the world. Augusta also heard that Haw was being considered as a candidate for a seat in the U.S. Senate. She wrote her husband a letter saying that she wanted to attend the opening night of the new opera house with him. Furthermore, she hoped to go with him to

Washington as a senator's wife. It is not known whether or how Haw answered the letter, but on opening night, September 5, 1881, the Tabors' opera box was empty.

Augusta then made an unusual move. On April 19, 1882, she brought a bill of complaint against her husband in which she sued him for $50,000 a year in alimony, even though they were not divorced. Publicity from this lawsuit caused considerable damage to Haw's reputation and to his hopes for a political future. The suit was finally thrown out of court and, although Haw's good name had been tarnished and public sympathy lay mostly with Augusta, it was she who was ultimately losing the power struggle. The following month, Augusta gave in and sold her interest in the Windsor Hotel to the Tabors' partner, Bill Bush.

For nearly three years, Augusta did everything she could to avoid divorce. She seemed to think that if she waited patiently, Haw would come to his senses and recognize his responsibility to her and their son. But Haw was equally determined to divorce Augusta and marry Baby Doe. Finally, on January 2, 1883, Augusta granted a divorce to Haw in exchange for property worth about $300,000, though she stated during the court proceedings that she was not acting willingly.

Haw did not walk away from the experience unscathed. The scandal and subsequent divorce thwarted his political aspirations. The Colorado legislature offered him only a thirty-day interim term to fill in for Senator Henry Teller while they chose a replacement. In January 1883 Haw went to Washington, where he made the most of his temporary status as a U.S. senator. On March 1, just before his term expired, he staged an elaborate wedding for himself and Baby Doe. The guest list contained the names of numerous Washington bigwigs, including the president himself, Chester Arthur. Many people however, especially the wives, refused to attend. Haw was never nominated for another major political position.

After the marriage, Haw and his new wife returned to Denver. The city's social elite openly spurned the new Mrs. Tabor, often referring to her simply as "that blonde." Augusta, on the other hand, was embraced and showered with sympathy. Upon returning from a trip to California, she was welcomed back into Denver society with a surprise party attended by 250 guests.

A *Denver Republican* reporter interviewed Augusta in October 1883. The interview was conducted in her elegant twenty-room mansion, part of her divorce settlement from the Silver King. It was clear that Augusta could not reconcile herself to being divorced. In the interview she said, "I don't consider myself divorced from Mr. Tabor. The whole proceedings were irregular. If it were not for my son, Maxcy, I would commence suit tomorrow to have the divorce annulled. I repeat, it was illegal." When asked about her ex-husband's new wife, Augusta replied coolly, "She is a blonde, I understand, and paints [her face]. I have never seen her."

Augusta clung to the belief that Haw's second wife was nothing more than a gold digger who would leave him if he ran out of money. She continued to stay in the house she and Haw had lived in and bided her time, hoping Haw would return to her one day. In the meantime, she remained active in Denver, contributing to the United Unitarian Church of Denver as well as the Catholic Church and sometimes hosting fundraisers in her mansion. She also worked with the Pioneer Ladies' Aid Society, which supported Denver's women's hospital, orphanage, and free kindergarten.

In 1892 Augusta finally sold her house and moved temporarily into the Brown Palace Hotel. The following year, financial disaster struck Horace Tabor. The silver panic of 1893 ruined him, yet Baby Doe did not leave him as Augusta and so many others had predicted.* Augusta finally realized that Haw was not coming back to her.

---

*Haw Tabor would die a poor man in 1899, and Baby Doe would live thirty-five more years in poverty and, some said, madness.

Always financially savvy, Augusta remained wealthy even as her former husband lost everything. But her health had begun to fail. Suffering from a persistent cough and other complaints, she moved to Pasadena, California, to take advantage of the milder climate.

Augusta's health did not improve in sunny California, however. She died at the Balmoral Hotel in Pasadena on February 1, 1895, at age sixty-two. The doctor listed her cause of death as chronic bronchitis and pneumonia. Maxcy Tabor brought his mother's body back to Denver for burial. Augusta's funeral, held at the Unitarian Church she had so generously supported, was crowded beyond capacity.

Speaking at Augusta Tabor's funeral, Reverend N. A. Haskell said, "Perhaps there is not even a man in the state who has done so much to open the way into the wilderness as she who lies here."

Chief Ouray and wife Chipeta, Washington, D.C., 1880
—Courtesy Western History Collection, Denver Public Library

4

CHIPETA

Native American Peacemaker

Chipeta galloped from the Ute camp into the mountains to find her husband, Chief Ouray, to tell him the terrible news: Indian agent Nathan Meeker had been murdered, along with ten other white men. She knew how desperately the chief's influence was going to be needed to avoid bloody retribution.

It was late September of 1879, and tensions between the White River Utes and white soldiers and settlers in Colorado had erupted. The tribe, angry that the government had not delivered on promises agreed to in recent treaties, made raids on white settlements and stole horses. At the White River Indian Agency, agent Nathan Meeker was expected to handle the situation, but the Utes were already fed up with Meeker and his efforts to force them to give up their land and their way of life and become Christian farmers. After an argument one day, Meeker threatened the Indians with military action. Enraged, the Utes returned later that day and attacked the agency, killing Meeker and his employees and kidnapping three white women and two children.

Ouray was the leader of the Uncompahgre Utes, a band related to the White River Utes. He was known as a diplomat between the Utes and the government. Upon their arrival at the Uncompahgre village, Ouray and Chipeta were met by former Indian agent Charles Adams, a man they knew well. He spoke with Ouray and Chipeta into the night. They agreed that their only hope of preventing a massive reprisal upon the Utes was to quickly rescue the captives. Ouray contacted the chief of the White River Utes, Chief Douglas, and insisted that the captives be released immediately. The women and children were freed and taken to Ouray's adobe house.

With tears of sympathy on her face, Chipeta ran out to meet the traumatized captives as they rode up. She welcomed them into her home for the night, feeding them and making them warm and comfortable. She held the children and soothed them with gentle songs. The victims later reported that Chipeta had treated them like her own family. It was a bright and tender encounter after twenty-three days of terror and suffering.

Chipeta, whose name translates as "White Singing Bird," was a Kiowa Apache believed to have been born in the summer of 1843. When she was only two years old, her parents were killed by raiders from another tribe, and Chipeta was found in the desolate camp the next day, wandering amid her slain family members. It was members of the Uncompahgre Utes who found her, and they brought her into their tribe. From that moment on, she was considered a Ute. She grew up with an older brother named Sapovanero and a younger brother named John McCook.

Ute families did not stay in one place but roamed a large territory, camping according to the seasons. In winter, a small number of families might camp together in a valley of the San Juan Mountains, which provided some protection from the fierce winter wind and snow. Since game was hard to find in winter, making it difficult to support more than a few families, Ute bands spread out further in the cold months. Once winter passed, the scattered families came together in one place and celebrated the coming of spring with the Bear Dance ceremony.

During the summer months, the Utes fished, picked wild berries, and gathered edible plants, seeds, and bulbs. They enjoyed some of these foods fresh, then dried the rest for later, saving as much as they could to help them survive the next winter. Come autumn, Ute families joined together in South Park for the buffalo hunt. The buffalo supplied meat as well as shelters, clothing, blankets, fuel, glue, rope, weapons, utensils, tools, and more. The Utes dried some of the buffalo meat and added it to their winter stores.

One year, a young Uncompahgre Ute man named Ouray ("Arrow") joined Chipeta's band in a winter camp. Ouray, who was half Jicarilla Apache, had grown up in present-day New Mexico, then part of Mexico, and spoke four languages—Apache, Ute, Spanish, and English. Ouray's father, Guerra Murah, was a Ute chief who had moved to Colorado a few years before, and Ouray joined him there after attending a white school in Taos, New Mexico.

Young Ouray became a respected hunter in his adopted band. He married Black Mare, a friend of Chipeta's, and the couple had a son, Queashegut, nicknamed Parone. When Black Mare died, while Parone was still a baby, young Chipeta stepped in to care for the child. In 1859, when she turned sixteen, Chipeta married Ouray, age twenty-six, and she raised Parone as her own son. A year later, Ouray's father died, and Ouray became a Ute chief. Before long, he became known as the "Peace Chief" for his dedication to keeping the peace with white people.

Even as the wife of a chief, Chipeta did the regular work of women of the tribe, such as tanning hides, sewing clothes and moccasins, drying meat, cooking, and hauling water. She was known for her fine beadwork, with which she decorated clothing, moccasins, and cradleboards; she would continue this art into her old age.

Another major responsibility for Ute women was motherhood and child care. Chipeta never had children of her own, but she had Parone, and later, she and Ouray adopted three orphans. Utes commonly took in children who had lost their parents. According to Ute custom, Chipeta's inability to bear children gave Ouray reason to divorce her. But Ouray loved his wife, and he not only stayed with her but took her into his confidence on matters both private and public. It was unusual for a man, especially a chief, to show a woman such trust and respect. The Utes, in turn, held Chipeta in high regard.

Because of her position, Chipeta was allowed in council meetings, which no other women attended. Chipeta assisted her husband in all his peacekeeping endeavors. They both believed that the white people were too strong to resist, and that if the Utes were to survive, they would have to find a way to peacefully coexist.

Many issues put the Native Americans at odds with settlers and with the U.S. government. Before the Civil War, small groups of farmers and prospectors had come west and began to claim land that had traditionally been Indian hunting grounds. After the war, more settlers arrived to claim homesteads and more gold and silver miners came to dig around for ore, leading to increasing conflicts between the immigrants and the natives. Faced with this pressure, Ouray recommended negotiating with, rather than fighting, the government. He tried to make the best treaties that he could for his people, but the government constantly broke the agreements, and many Utes understandably did not trust white leaders.

Some Uncompahgre Utes supported Chief Ouray, but he was only one of many Ute chiefs, and other chiefs and tribal members disagreed with his beliefs and actions. While the government considered Ouray a spokesman for the Utes because of his education and his friendly relationships with whites, the Utes themselves never chose him to speak for them or make decisions on behalf of the whole tribe. Thus many Utes resented him.

In fact, on one occasion, Chipeta's own brother, Sapavanero, tried to kill Ouray. Sapavanero hid inside the blacksmith's shop at the Los Pinos Agency and waited to ambush his brother-in-law with an ax. The blacksmith, however, alerted Ouray to the danger, and the two

Utes got into a scuffle. Finally, Ouray got the upper hand and held Sapavanero at knifepoint. The chief would have killed his brother-in-law if Chipeta had not intervened. Frightened and distressed, she scolded them both, saying how much their violent enmity hurt her. She asked both men to promise never to hurt each other, and they agreed. Over time, Ouray and Sapavanero became trusted friends.

Ouray's first major opportunity to negotiate a treaty occurred when the Colorado Territory was organized in 1861. At the urging of his old friend from Taos, Kit Carson, Ouray went to Denver to meet with territorial governor John Evans, who proposed that a treaty council be held between the United States government and the Utes. In February 1863, Ouray and a small delegation of Utes traveled to Washington, D.C., to meet with President Lincoln. Ouray was away for many months, while Chipeta stayed at home with Parone.

Upon his return in June, Ouray rode all over Colorado to meet with the scattered Ute bands. President Lincoln had asked him to gather representatives from the various Ute groups to meet with government officials in October. Ouray invited all the Ute chiefs to send representatives to the October council. But before that meeting took place, Ouray was to face a personal tragedy.

One day Ouray took Parone, then about six years old, with him on a hunting trip with a small party of Ute men. While the hunters were camped, a band of Sioux raiders attacked the camp and kidnapped Parone. Ouray and Chipeta were heartbroken. For years afterward, Ouray searched for his son, to no avail. He later heard that the Sioux had given Parone to some Arapahos. In 1872 Ouray enlisted the government to help him locate his boy. Officials found a teenager they believed was Parone living with the Arapahos, but when Ouray met him, neither he nor the boy believed they were father and son. The mystery was never solved.

On October 1, 1863, the still grief-stricken Ouray attended the great council between the Uncompahgre Utes and Lincoln's representatives at Conejos, Colorado. On the seventh day of meet-ings, nine Ute chiefs, including Ouray, signed a treaty. The agree-ment gave a section of Ute land to the government in exchange for a number of horses, cattle, and sheep as well as food and household goods to be provided every year for ten years. The rest of the land would be reserved for the Utes, and the government promised to protect the tribal land from prospectors and settlers who tried to claim it.

Ouray's leadership at the treaty council impressed the white offi-cials, and they entrusted him with increased responsibilities. Soon Chipeta found herself in a lonely position. Ouray was constantly being sent off to negotiate between the government and the Ute bands, so he was seldom around, and her son, who used to occupy her days, was gone. Chipeta asked her husband if she could travel with him, and knowing how much he relied on her contributions, he readily agreed. Now Chipeta would play a bigger role in white-Indian peacekeeping than any other Native American woman of her time.

As Ouray and Chipeta traveled to various Ute camps, Chipeta mingled with other tribal members, who spoke freely to her. The information she shared with her husband helped him make thought-ful decisions. With Chipeta's help, Ouray gained a reputation for fairness and wisdom.

As was the case with so many treaties between Indian tribes and the government, the United States did not honor the terms of the 1863 treaty with the Utes. The promised food and supplies were not deliv-ered, and miners roamed all over the Utes' reserved lands looking for silver and gold. Conflicts arose, and now Colorado's new governor, A. Cameron Hunt, and many other whites wanted the Utes completely removed from the state.

Chipeta accompanied Ouray to Washington for another treaty conference in 1868. The new treaty ceded more Ute land to the United States and created an Indian agency for the Uncompahgre, the Los Pinos Agency, in Conejos. Here Ouray, with Chipeta at his side, continued to serve as interpreter and mediator.

In 1872 gold was discovered in the San Juan Mountains, creating a new stream of prospectors and businesses in the area, including the Uncompahgre Utes' remaining territory. More clashes erupted, and in 1875 the government moved the Los Pinos Agency to the Uncompahgre Valley, on the western slope of the Colorado Rockies.

By this time Chipeta and Ouray were subject to increasing mistrust among their own people. Not only did they give up more and more Ute land to the government, they also received special favors and lived differently from the majority of Utes. They were given a large house on a three-hundred-acre farm near the new agency and received $500 to $1,000 a year for Ouray's role as mediator. Although she lived in the government house, Chipeta insisted she preferred her teepee.

It was at this government house that Chipeta welcomed the five captives from the 1879 attack on the Meeker agency. One of the rescued women, Flora Ellen Price, was later called to testify in Washington about what had happened. She had nothing but good things to say about Chipeta. "We were treated well at Ouray's house.... We were received as old friends. Mrs. Ouray wept for our hardships and her motherly face, dusky but beautiful, with sweetness and compassion, was wet with tears."

In January of 1880, President Rutherford Hayes invited Ouray to make another trip to Washington, D.C., to discuss yet another treaty, and Chipeta again accompanied him. It was not a happy trip. By this time, Chief Ouray was seriously ill with kidney disease. Furthermore, both Ouray and Chipeta knew that they could not stop the white man from taking over the rest of their land. If the government could not get the land by treaty, they would take it by force. All the Utes could hope for was a safe place to live.

At the council, Ouray did his best to persuade government officials to allow the Utes to continue living in Colorado, but it was no use. Because he had little choice, Ouray signed over everything the Utes had left—encompassing millions of acres of Colorado grassland—and agreed that the tribe would move to a reservation on desert land in eastern Utah Territory.

After Ouray concluded the treaty, he returned home to die. He went to an encampment where nearly a thousand Utes from seven bands had gathered. Chipeta nursed her husband as he passed in and out of consciousness, staying with him until his last breath. After Ouray's death, Chipeta cut her hair as a sign of mourning, and the Utes sang death songs to guide the chief's spirit to the other side. Ouray's body was wrapped and taken away to a place the white men would not know about.

In September 1881, a year after Ouray's death, the U.S. cavalry escorted 1,458 Uncompahgre Utes from Colorado to the Utah reservation. Chipeta had originally expected to be allowed to stay in her government-built home at Los Pinos, but the government sold the house, farm, and all the livestock immediately after Ouray's death. Government officials promised to build her a new home at the Utah reservation, but when she arrived there, Chipeta found it was nothing more than a crudely built, unfurnished two-room cabin. Insulted, she chose to live in her own teepee instead.

Chipeta and the other Utes did their best to adjust to their new life in a strange place. Chipeta's camp on the reservation included her brother, John McCook, and other family members. In summer, they moved a short distance off the reservation to graze their sheep in western Colorado. In winter, Chipeta and John returned to the Utah reservation to camp along Bitter Creek. A few years later, Chipeta remarried. Her new husband was a Ute named Accumooquats, and the couple adopted several orphans.

Chipeta found herself caught up in another conflict in 1887. One day, a few Ute raiders stole some horses from a local rancher in Garfield County, and the sheriff went out after them with a posse of cowboys. At the time, Chipeta along with five other women and eight children were staying at their camp tending the sheep herds while the men, including Chipeta's husband and brother, were away hunting. The cowboys entered Chipeta's camp and began to taunt and threaten the women and children. Chipeta, pointing out that she and the others had no horses and so clearly weren't horse thieves, demanded that the intruders leave. They did so, but Chipeta feared they might return. As soon as the posse was out of sight, she led the women and children up the mountainside to hide.

Chipeta at her teepee, Ute reservation in Utah, circa 1923
—Courtesy Western History Collection, Denver Public Library

As Chipeta had suspected, some of the cowboys returned. These rowdies looted the camp and burned some of the teepees. Seeing this, Chipeta made the decision to abandon their sheep and flee. As she was leading the women and children toward another Ute camp to the north, the cowboys spotted them and chased after them. Fortunately, the sheriff returned and stopped his unruly men, scolding them that they were supposed to be hunting horse thieves, not women and children.

Chipeta's ordeal was not over, however. As the news of the horse theft spread, it escalated into wild rumors that the Utes were burning and looting settlers' homes. In response to the perceived threat, the governor, Benjamin Eaton, sent out the militia. All Utes were warned to return immediately to their reservation. Chipeta and the others made the difficult walk back to their camp, where they found that their sheep and most of their other possessions had been stolen or destroyed. An investigation into the matter revealed that the cowboy posses had used the excuse of the Ute raid to cover their own thievery. They had taken 600 horses, 37 cows, and 2,300 sheep and goats from Utes in the area.

Government officials promised to return the Utes' livestock and property to them, but they received only a small number of goats and sheep. Special Agent H. S. Welton was sent to the reservation a year later to discuss the damages, and Chipeta was one of the thirty Utes to meet with him. Although she was not officially a chief, her opinion was still valued. The government promised to pay the Utes $32,000 for the stolen livestock, but, as usual, the money was never received. A few years later, adding to the Utes' misery, a diphtheria epidemic struck the reservation in 1890. It is believed that Chipeta's second husband probably died of the disease.

In 1898 the government assigned allotments of land to individual Utes rather than to the tribe as a whole. Chipeta claimed 160 arid acres on the White River, and her brother, John McCook, took

160 acres on Bitter Creek. The Indian agent suggested that the Utes brand their sheep to protect them from further theft. With these meager resources, Chipeta and her tribespeople eked out a living.

Chipeta continued to be an influential member of the tribe and was often consulted in tribal matters. The new agent made a written record of Chipeta's participation in the Council of Chiefs in 1910. She spoke briefly, saying that the government had failed to keep its promises. She is quoted as saying, "These sheep men tell their herders this land does not belong to the Indians."

By the early 1900s, Chipeta, still honored as a wise woman of the tribe, was growing old and living in poverty. Hearing of this, some of her old white friends in Colorado checked in on her in Utah and brought her back to Colorado for a visit. They took her around in an automobile to show her the "improvements" that had been made since she left. Her friends also lobbied legislators to create a special fund to help support her. Their efforts failed, but the publicity brought Chipeta's name before the public again.

In 1909 Chipeta was invited to the dedication ceremony for the newly built Gunnison Tunnel, which had been drilled through the mountains to bring water to the Uncompahgre Valley. On her way to the ceremony in Montrose, she stopped in Grand Junction, where President William Howard Taft was speaking. She was introduced to the president, who insisted that she ride with him in his private railcar to Montrose.

Chipeta visited Colorado again in 1911, attending the Fourth of July celebration in Montrose and several other events held around the state at which she was received as an honored guest. While Chipeta was pleased to be remembered by people in Colorado, it did not make up for her poor treatment by the U.S. government. Yet she never became bitter.

Around 1916 the Commissioner of Indian Affairs wanted to send Chipeta a gift of appreciation for all she had done. Rather than give her something of real value, however, all he sent her was a shawl. She not only accepted it graciously but sent him a saddle blanket in return, along with a note saying, "I am glad there is no more trouble between the Indians and the white people, and hope that this state of affairs exists through the rest of my life time."

In her old age, Chipeta's eyesight was very poor, but she continued to travel a little with her brother, John McCook, often riding on a train. At one point she visited Glenwood Springs, Colorado, pointing out to some of the guests there that she and Ouray had soaked in the springs long before the white man came.

Chipeta died on August 16, 1924, at age eighty-one. A headline in the *Denver Post* read, "Queen Chipeta Rejoins Husband, Chief Ouray, in Happy Hunting Ground." She was buried according to Ute custom in a ravine near Bitter Creek.

After her death, various groups wanted Chipeta's remains to be returned to Colorado, including the Montrose Chapter of the Daughters of the American Revolution. The group had recently built a memorial to her, in the form of a concrete teepee, at the farm where she and Ouray had lived at Los Pinos Agency. They proposed reburying her there, and Chipeta's brother, John McCook, agreed to the move.

Chipeta's remains were taken by train from Dragon, Utah, to Montrose on March 14, 1925. From there, Chipeta's brother and others accompanied her coffin in a four-mile procession to Ouray Springs. That afternoon, 5,000 people gathered at the burial site to watch her coffin be placed in an open vault. The observances included both an Indian ceremony and a Christian service.

Interested parties, including John McCook, then expressed the desire to have Chief Ouray's remains removed from their secret burial place and placed next to Chipeta. A council of Ute chiefs agreed to move the remains, but not to the farm site. They decided instead to rebury Ouray at the reservation cemetery, which would be renamed Ouray Memorial Cemetery. A huge memorial service was held on May 24, 1925, for the reburial. In 1939 a massive monument was built nearby in memory of Ouray and other famous Ute leaders.

Attempts to have Chipeta's remains moved once again to the cemetery next to Ouray were unsuccessful. However, a stone obelisk inset with a bronze portrait of Ouray was placed near Chipeta's grave. Their old farm site was made into a public park, named Ouray Memorial Park. Chipeta's brother, John McCook, is buried here, too, and the park has been expanded to include the Ute Indian Museum and a native plants garden.

In 1985 Chipeta was inducted into the Colorado Women's Hall of Fame for the "courage and valor she demonstrated in her efforts to mediate between Native Americans and whites."

Portrait of Mary Elitch Long, 1896
—Courtesy Colorado Historical Society

5

MARY ELITCH LONG

Gracious Lady of the Gardens

Daisy, one of a small group of bears that lived in the Elitch Zoological Gardens in Denver, escaped unnoticed from the bear pen and made her way to Mary Elitch's cottage on the garden grounds. When Mary came home, Daisy was standing happily at the kitchen counter playing with the water faucets that she had cleverly managed to turn on.

On entering her cottage and seeing the bear, Mary fled for the door, but she was not quick enough. The bear caught her and with her big paws pinned Mary against the dining room sideboard.

Mary knew she was in a bad spot, but she managed to stay calm and think fast. She slowly reached for the sugar bowl on the shelf beside her and dropped it on the floor, then with one foot kicked the bowl away as far as she could.

The plan worked. Daisy immediately dropped down to the floor to get at the sugar, and Mary raced to the door and slammed it behind her. A tragedy was averted and Mary could add another incident to her pamphlet, "Experiences of the Only Woman in the World Who Owns and Manages a Zoo."

Mary Elizabeth Hauck, usually called Lydia by her family members, was born on May 10, 1856, in Philadelphia, Pennsylvania, the eldest of six children. When she was almost three, her family moved to a farm in California, not far from San Francisco, where Mary attended a Roman Catholic convent school.

In 1872, when she was sixteen, Mary met a handsome twenty-two-year-old man at church named John Elitch, Jr. John had grown up in Alabama and moved to San Francisco, where he found work in restaurants in the theater district. The two fell in love. Mary's parents thought their daughter was much too young for marriage, so the love-struck couple eloped. On their honeymoon, John took Mary to see her first play, *The Streets of New York*.

Eight years later, in 1880, Mary and John moved to Colorado to open a restaurant in Durango. It was a success, and they used their profits to move to the thriving young city of Denver, where they opened a bigger restaurant, the Elitch Palace Dining Room, two years later. The new business flourished, serving Denver VIPs from politics, business, and entertainment. John and Mary became prominent members of the community. With some of his customers and friends, John helped form the Denver Athletic Club.

Although she and John had no children, Mary kept more than busy. Besides the restaurant, she had three other passions: animals, art, and gardening. She was constantly bringing home stray cats and dogs, and she loved to paint, joining the Denver Art Club. But she had little room to garden. In 1888 the Elitches bought a sixteen-acre farm and orchard, the Chilcott Farm, five miles northwest of Denver, where Mary could keep as many animals as she wanted and plant flowers and vegetables to her heart's content.

The Elitches' new place included an old farmhouse, sprawling grounds with majestic old trees, and an immense apple orchard. Mary soon added a huge vegetable garden, raising some of the food that she and John served in their restaurant. She also planted all sorts of shrubs and flowers, patterned after a favorite park in San Francisco, and before long she had a beautiful, flourishing garden.

By this time, the Elitches also owned a considerable menagerie. The famous circus owner P. T. Barnum had given them some baby circus animals to care for, in addition to their other animals. Among their charges were lion cubs, an ostrich, and even a dancing bear. Mary and John began to wonder if they should open their home to the public. They came up with an exciting idea: Why not combine the gardens, the animals, and a restaurant in a single attraction? The Elitches sold the Palace Dining Room and set to work on their new dream.

In addition to the beautiful plantings and the animals, John and Mary built a children's playground, attractive picnic spots, an athletic field, and booths selling sodas and sweets. The Elitches' new restaurant, the Orchard Café, would serve delightful dishes made with fresh produce. And because of John's acting background, he naturally wanted to include a theater as part of the offerings at the gardens. He and Mary began planning an open-air theater, which they called a "theatorium," in which they intended to present all sorts of vaudeville acts, music, and plays. Although many similar parks featured beer gardens, Mary did not allow alcohol in Elitch Gardens, emphasizing her park's wholesome family atmosphere.

The grand opening of Elitch's Zoological Gardens was set for May 1, 1890. It turned out to be a very rainy day, and the Elitches feared that no one would come. But they need not have worried—people came in droves from Denver and from out of town. Among the famous visitors on opening day were silver king H.A.W. Tabor and the Elitches' friend P. T. Barnum, who brought with him the famous Tom Thumb, the world's smallest man. The mayor of Denver made the opening remarks. Marching bands played, and families were delighted with the children's activities, which included pony rides and a play area with swings and teeter-totters. Mary proudly drove around the grounds in a small cart pulled by the ostrich.

The first summer was a stunning success. By the time they closed for the season on Labor Day, the Elitches had earned an unbelievable $35,000. John took some of the profits to organize a small theater troupe, the Goodyear, Elitch, & Schilling Minstrels, planning to spend the winter months touring up and down the West Coast.

A few months into the troupe's first winter tour, while performing in San Francisco, John contracted pneumonia. His condition worsened, and he died two weeks later, on March 10, 1891, at age forty. Mary was thirty-four. She was devastated by the loss of her cherished husband of nearly nineteen years, but she was a strong woman and resolved to move on with her life.

In John's memory, and for her own sake, Mary decided to keep going with the Zoological Gardens, but she didn't have enough money. To raise funds, she sold some stock in the gardens to a group of Denver capitalists, though she maintained control of the business operations. The park continued to see success, and Mary was able to buy back the stock only three years later, regaining total control of her beloved enterprise.

The Elitch Theatre opened in 1892, the year after John's death. John had designed it based on Shakespeare's Globe Theatre in England, with eight sides and a domed roof. He had begun construction during their first season, and Mary completed it during the second summer. Early offerings included vaudeville and variety acts. Later Mary added full-length plays and light opera as well as music concerts. Music was an important attraction at the gardens. The Elitch Gardens Orchestra was Denver's first symphony orchestra. In addition to playing in the theater, the orchestra presented outdoor concerts on Friday afternoons.

Besides running the theater and gardens, Mary devoted large amounts of time to her animals. She raised many of the babies by hand, including several lion cubs. When they grew too big for her to keep, she sent them off to larger zoos. Also included in the gardens were a number of native animals such as deer, elk, and buffalo. To her already extensive zoo she soon added a water buffalo, a camel, peacocks, elephants, a monkey, and a kangaroo. She also had a number of bears. One of them, called Sam, had been trained to perform in the circus. Mary sometimes entertained the crowd by waltzing with Sam the Dancing Bear. A female seal in her collection gave birth to the first baby seal born in an American zoo. Mary held a contest to name the mother and baby, who ended up being called Celia and Cellina. When the Denver Zoo opened in 1896, Mary donated most of her animals to that better equipped facility, keeping only a few pets and special animals at the gardens.

In 1896 the Elitch Theatre made history when it presented the first motion picture ever seen in the American West, played on Thomas Edison's Vitascope, which projected sequenced images onto a large screen. Mary also adopted another invention of Edison's, electric lights, to light the gardens at night. The lights attracted insects, inspiring Mary some years later to write a children's book, *The Moth and the Moon*, published in 1924, about the moths that flew into the lights and died.

In 1897 Mary hired a local daredevil named Ivy Baldwin to perform. His act featured a huge balloon called an aerostat, two hundred feet in circumference, which when filled with gas rose to 1,500 feet. Baldwin made parachute jumps from the tethered craft to amaze the crowd. Later, guests were lifted up in the balloon's large basket, made of willow reeds, to enjoy views of the countryside. Some people even held their wedding ceremonies in the balloon at Elitch Gardens.

Meanwhile, Mary made improvements on the Elitch Theatre and, with the help of her late husband's theater friends, expanded its offerings to include full-length dramatic plays. The opening production in 1897 starred celebrated actor James O'Neill (father of future playwright Eugene O'Neill), who had promised John Elitch he would appear in his theater one day. For this show, Mary had hired a fourteen-year-old boy named Douglas as a stagehand. The boy had been hanging around the theater since he was twelve, doing odd jobs in exchange for tickets to the shows. Young Douglas Fairbanks grew up to be one of the most famous stage and movie actors of his time.

When the park closed at the end of each summer, Mary went to New York and San Francisco to find new plays and actors for her Denver audiences. Because she offered theater stars as much money to perform at Elitch Gardens as they would earn on Broadway, her theater always boasted the latest and greatest in theatrical entertainment. Among the stars who appeared at Elitch Gardens were Sarah Bernhardt, the most famous actress of her day; legendary Hollywood director Cecil B. DeMille; silent movie star Harold Lloyd; and, years later, film superstars Grace Kelly and Robert Redford, along with dozens of others.

In 1899, the very busy Mary hired a manager to help her run the playhouse, a widower named Thomas D. Long. Working together, Mary and Thomas became close friends. Within a year, their friendship blossomed into romance, and in 1900, they were married in a cottage on the garden grounds.

The newlyweds left on a six-month trip around the world. They were entertained by theater celebrities in Vienna, Berlin, Paris, Calcutta, and Tokyo. The couple also visited many amusement parks in Europe, gathering ideas for improving Elitch Gardens. There they saw interesting mechanical amusement rides such as carousels, trolley rides, and roller coasters, convincing Mary and Thomas to add some rides to the gardens.

On their return to Denver, Mary and her husband had a long list of improvements for Elitch Gardens. First they set to work remodeling and enlarging the theater. Later, one of Mary's friends, Margaret Fealy, started the Elitch School of Drama, which attracted promising young talent to Denver. Antoinette Perry, the famous Broadway director and producer for whom the Tony Awards were named, launched her career at Elitch Gardens in 1904, at age eleven.

Mary's next priority was to acquire some amusement rides for the park. Luna Park in New York's Coney Island already had a Toboggan Figure 8 Coaster Ride, which Mary enthusiastically rode during a trip to New York City. After her first ride, she immediately knew Elitch Gardens had to have one, too. She had the roller coaster installed in time for opening day in 1904. It was a huge hit, and Mary was rapidly becoming known as the "First Lady of Fun."

Mary also ordered two other rides: a carousel and a miniature train. The steam-powered miniature train, which took two years to build, ran on twelve-inch-wide tracks. Installed around 1905, it had eight cars, each of which could carry three or four children. The popular little railroad carried up to 15,000 passengers a day. The carousel, specially ordered from the Philadelphia Toboggan Company, took three years to carve, arriving in 1906. This one-of-a-kind ride featured not only horses, but forty-six different animals, including a giraffe, a hippo, and lions. The carver added wonderful details like real horns on the deer and real horsehair for the horses' tails. In the center of this remarkable carousel was a Wurlitzer organ that had 255 pipes, drums, and cymbals. When a new carousel replaced it in 1928, the original was sold to Kit Carson County, Colorado, where it still operates today at the county fairgrounds in Burlington.

Throughout the early 1900s, Elitch Gardens continued to evolve. Around 1909 an ornate new stucco entrance gate replaced the old log entryway. By 1910 Mary had also added a floating garden, the only one of its kind in the country, to her growing amusement park. She had dreamt up the design, which featured flowers floating in lighted pools, during the winter months. Thomas, too, spent much time working on the gardens. He designed flowerbeds and worked in the greenhouses, raising flowers and other plants not only for the gardens but also for sale to Denver landscapers. Recognized as a expert in park landscape design, he became a member of the Denver Parks board of directors in 1912.

In 1910 Mary launched one of her most ambitious projects. She built a special new theater in which to stage a reenactment of the famous Civil War battle between the warships the *USS Monitor* and the *USS Merrimac* (which had actually been renamed the *CSS Virginia*). The show was billed as a $200,000 naval spectacle. The stage was two hundred feet long, one hundred feet deep, and five feet high, and the ships were life-size. The producers used lots of special effects that amazed their audiences. Unfortunately, only four years later, the theater burned to the ground. Because of the great cost involved, it was not rebuilt.

Visitors roam in front of Long residence at Elitch Gardens, early 1900s
—Courtesy Western History Collection, Denver Public Library

An advertisement that appeared in the 1910s reflected the growing importance of Elitch Gardens: it read "Not to see Elitch's is not to see Denver." Later this slogan was spelled out in flowers near the park's entrance. It was truly the park's golden age, as Elitch Gardens kept getting better and better.

Shortly after the gardens opened, Mary had designated Tuesday as Children's Day. She organized classes in drama, folk dance, arts and crafts, and other subjects. She also held various contests, in which she usually took an active part. In addition to entertaining the youngsters, Mary also wanted to teach them about nature. She wrote a series of booklets about the various animals—their natural habitats, what they ate, and how they lived—and gave them away to her young zoo visitors. She also published a weekly newspaper for kids, the *Child's Companion*, which had a circulation of 15,000.

During the early 1900s, each Children's Day drew about 3,000 youngsters, with assistants to help manage the young crowds. The program boasted that not a single child had been hurt during Children's Day. On other special days, free admissions were made available for orphanages, Sunday schools, and old folks' homes. In addition, Mary helped the Denver community by hosting special fundraisers at the gardens, with the money taken in going to worthy charities.

Mary's generous nature eventually caused her financial difficulties. With her charity events and free-admission days the gardens were not taking in enough money to cover expenses. Bills became overdue, and investors in the company worried. Before long, Mary had no choice but to sell Elitch Gardens.

The first buyer to appear on the scene was the Sells Flotto Circus. They proposed to close the garden to the public and use the area for their winter home. The citizens of Denver were most unhappy with this prospect, and a group was organized called the Friends of the Gardens. The Friends put on a big benefit to help Mary keep the park, but although it brought in a lot of money, the amount was not sufficient to cover the debts.

In 1916 Elitch Gardens was sold to a group of Denver businessmen, who agreed to keep the park open and not to change the name. The group hired John Mulvihill, the money manager for the Denver Gas & Electric Company, to run the park. Mulvihill paid all the bills and taxes and later bought out the other investors. He closed the gardens for a season to work on improvements. John Mulvihill loved the gardens, and he wanted to keep Mary involved. He allowed her to stay at the gardens and live for free in her cottage for as long as she wished, and she always had reserved seats at the theater. Later, a new stucco house was built for Mary at the gardens. Throughout her years there, she often had friends come to visit and attend the theater with her.

Mary provided vision for the gardens while John Mulvihill managed the business affairs carefully. The park reopened in 1917 with a new attraction: the Trocadero Ballroom. With its huge, open-air dance floor, the "Troc" became a very popular spot, with live bands and dancing in the evenings as well as afternoon tea dances in which the ladies wore lovely dresses and white gloves. A succession of famous bandleaders played there over the years, including Benny Goodman, Tommy Dorsey, Guy Lombardo, Gene Krupa, and Lawrence Welk.

In 1920 Mary was widowed again when Thomas Long was killed in a car accident on a mountain road. After her husband's death, Mary continued to devote her time and energy to the park, especially to the amusement rides. The seventy-five-foot-high Wildcat roller coaster debuted in 1922. Six years later, the beautiful new carousel was installed. This specially made carousel boasted sixty-four hand-carved animals, no two alike. The animals went up and down as the carousel revolved and music played. Restored several times over the years, this carousel still operates today at Elitch Gardens Theme Park.

In 1925 the Denver Women's Press Club hosted a special birthday party for Mary, at which she was honored for all she had done for the city. The mayor of Denver and the governor of Colorado, among others, were in attendance at the event. The club also awarded Mary, the "Lady of the Gardens," a lifetime honorary membership.

Mary was seventy-four when John Mulvihill died in 1930. He left the park to his son-in-law, Arnold Gurtler, who kept it open and continued to maintain it beautifully. The Gurtlers allowed Mary to stay on at her house in the gardens until 1932, when, because of failing health, she moved in with her sister-in-law. Elitch Gardens had been her home for forty years.

Mary Elitch Long died after a stroke on July 16, 1936, at age eighty. She was a truly beloved figure in the Denver community. A *Denver Post* editorial said: "Mary Elitch does not need a few passing words to make her glory complete." During her funeral at the Cathedral of the Immaculate Conception, Monsignor William F. O'Ryan compared Mary to St. Francis of Assissi, saying that "Both believed in the virtue of kindness, both knew and understood and drew the dumb creatures to them, casting out fear by gentleness and the speech that is of the spirit." She was buried next to John Elitch at Fairmount Cemetery in Denver.

Mary died with very little money or property. In her five-page, handwritten will, she left her few personal items to relatives, to her many friends, and to some of the children of Denver. Her true bequests were her vast contributions to the Denver community. In honor of her role in cultivating the performing arts in Denver, a chair at the Central City Opera House was later named for her. In 1996, sixty years after her death, Mary was inducted into both the Colorado Business Hall of Fame and the Colorado Women's Hall of Fame.

The Mulvihill-Gurtler family operated Elitch Gardens until 1994, when Sandy Gurtler sold the business, and the original park closed after 104 years. Many of the rides, including the magnificent carousel, were moved to the new Elitch Gardens amusement park, which was built about six miles from the original site. This became Six Flags Elitch Gardens in 1999, then Elitch Gardens Theme Park in 2006.

At the site of the original gardens is now a residential development called Highlands Garden Village, built in 1998. Though private homes cover most of the property, the Elitch Theatre, which underwent an extensive restoration in 2006, still stands and still operates at its original site. There is also a small park at the corner of the property called Mary Elitch Memorial Park, which includes a gazebo and a stone marker dedicated to Mary Elitch Long, the Lady of the Gardens.

Margaret Tobin Brown, circa 1895 —Courtesy
Western History Collection, Denver Public Library

6

MARGARET "MOLLY" BROWN

The Truth Behind the Legends

On April 18, 1912, reporters flocked to the pier as the *Carpathia* arrived in New York with 705 survivors from the *Titanic*, a luxury liner that had sunk three days earlier after hitting an iceberg in the North Sea. More than 1,500 passengers and crew members had perished in the icy waters. The reporters jockeyed for position along the docks, eager to get an interview with Mrs. J. J. Brown.

Word was already out that Margaret Brown was a heroine. Taking over Lifeboat Six, she shared her warm clothing with her fellow passengers, kept them rowing, and looked for survivors. Once aboard the rescue ship, she collected relief funds and helped organize medical help for many of the rescued passengers. Most of them were women, and many of them suddenly found themselves widowed, homeless, and without means of support.

Upon their arrival in New York, Margaret Brown did not remain ashore with the other first-class passengers. Eschewing the throngs of reporters, she returned to the *Carpathia,* saying, "God knows I can do little enough to save these poor souls around me that are out of their senses." She remained onboard another day to assist the needier women and children, many of whom could not speak English, find help from relatives, friends, the Red Cross, or the Travelers Aid Society. Because she spoke five foreign languages, she was able to communicate with most of the immigrants in their own tongue.

When Margaret finally spoke with reporters, she said, "Please don't say that I am a heroine. I did only the natural thing and not the heroic." In spite of her modesty, the stories that filled the nation's newspapers proclaimed her just that—the Heroine of the *Titanic*. When asked how she managed to survive, she replied lightheartedly, "Typical Brown luck. We're unsinkable."

Margaret Brown became an instant celebrity and, before long, a legend. She came to be known to history as the "Unsinkable Molly Brown."

Margaret Tobin was born on July 18, 1867, in Hannibal, Missouri, a small town of about 7,000 on the Mississippi River. Most of Margaret's friends and family called her Maggie; she was never known as Molly during her life. Maggie's father, John Tobin, worked as a laborer at the Hannibal Gas Works and was an ardent abolitionist. Her mother, Johanna, was a homemaker who also believed in equality for all. Both John and Johanna had been born in Ireland and had immigrated to America with family members. When they first met each other in Hannibal around 1861, both had recently been widowed and each had a young daughter.

The Tobin family lived in a small cottage on Denkler Alley, a section of Hannibal known as "Irish Town" because of the many Irish-Catholic immigrants who lived there. It was a poor, working-class neighborhood. Along with her two half-sisters (Catherine Tobin and Mary Ann Collins), Maggie had two brothers (Daniel and William) and a sister (Helen). Nearly everyone in the Tobin family was a redhead, but Maggie's hair was the reddest.

There were no formal schools in that part of Missouri at the time, so Margaret and her siblings, along with some of the other neighborhood children, took their lessons in the nearby home of Mary

O'Leary, one of Johanna Tobin's sisters. Maggie was an avid reader, and she also loved the outdoors. She enjoyed fishing and hiking along the Mississippi River and was considered a bit of a tomboy.

At the age of thirteen, Maggie took her first job to help support the family. She worked in the Garth Tobacco Factory, stripping tobacco leaves from their prickly stems. Child labor laws were nonexistent at the time; workers of all ages were on the job up to twelve hours a day, six days a week.

In 1883, after Maggie's half-sister, Mary Ann, married Jack Landrigan, Mary Ann and Jack left Missouri to try their luck in the silver mines of Colorado. Two years later Maggie's older brother, Daniel, went to join them out west, settling in Leadville, Colorado. Soon after, in the spring of 1886, nineteen-year-old Maggie and her fifteen-year-old sister, Helen, took a train to visit their brother.

At that time, Leadville, at an elevation of 10,000 feet, was the second-largest town in the ten-year-old state. Maggie decided to stay on in Colorado and keep house for her brother. She had always said she wanted to marry a rich man, and she hoped she might find one in the mining fields.

Wanting to help Daniel with expenses, Maggie found a job as a waitress and later worked in the carpet and drapes department at Daniels, Fisher & Smiths Emporium, a dry-goods store on the main street in Leadville. One day at church, she met an Irishman named James Joseph Brown, known as J.J. Brown, a mining engineer in his early thirties. He was tall and handsome but far from rich. Nevertheless, Maggie was in love.

After a six-month courtship, at age nineteen, Maggie Tobin became Mrs. J. J. Brown on September 1, 1886. Maggie and J.J. lived in a two-room cabin in Stumptown, a suburb of Leadville on Iron Hill. Stumptown got its name from the stumps of trees left from cutting timber for use in the mineshafts and for building cabins.

When the couple's son, Lawrence Palmer Brown (Larry), was born in 1887, the family moved into Leadville. Two years later, Maggie and J.J. had a second child, a daughter named Catherine Ellen, whom they called Helen after Maggie's little sister. Even as a busy new mother living in the rugged mining camps of Colorado, Maggie Brown was determined to expand her education. After all her work at the house was done, she took lessons from tutors in literature, piano, and singing.

In addition to her studies, Maggie took an active part in the Leadville community. Even though her husband was a manager, she sympathized with the struggling mine workers and helped them however she could. She organized soup kitchens and became involved in local and state politics, working for better schools and better health care for miners and their families. She also worked for women's suffrage in Colorado.

J.J. was no slacker, either. As the mining superintendent for the Ibex Mining Company, he developed a way to use hay bales to strengthen mine walls, which allowed mines to be built deeper, where gold ore could potentially be found. He also held part ownership in several of the mines. Using J.J.'s technique, one of them, the Little Jonny, hit gold in 1893, producing hundreds of tons of high-grade gold ore. The Browns were suddenly millionaires.

The following spring, the Brown family moved to Denver, buying a big house on Pennsylvania Avenue, in the Capitol Hill area. Unlike most homes in those days, the house had electricity, central heat, and hot and cold running water. Maggie, who had developed a passion for art, decorated her new home with paintings, sculptures, and rich, vibrant furnishings. After she put two large lion statues in front of the house, the place became known as the House of Lions.

Maggie's parents, who had moved to Colorado when Maggie's children were born and lived with them in Leadville, moved into the new house, too. Both lived with the Browns in Denver until their deaths. Maggie's father, John Tobin, died only a few years later, in 1899; her mother, Johanna, lived until 1905.

J.J. and Maggie also bought a ranch a few miles outside of town in what is now Lakewood, Colorado. Here the family went horseback riding, gardened, and raised chickens and some livestock. Maggie called the place Avoca Lodge, after a place called Avoca from one of her favorite poems by Sir Thomas Moore. The Browns spent summers at their ranch and winters in their town house.

Although the Browns were wealthy and often made news on the society pages, Maggie was not accepted into the elite circles of Denver society. Both J.J. and Maggie came from poor immigrant families, and at the time, the Irish in general were considered lowbrow. Maggie's red hair and flamboyant style, not to mention her progressive political views, did not help matters. In those days, Denver society was ruled by an exclusive group of conservative socialites sarcastically known as the "Sacred Thirty-Six," a group of three dozen women led by Mrs. Crawford Hill. They represented "old" money and "breeding" and wanted nothing to do with the flashy Mrs. J. J. Brown. J.J., however, was respected for his wealth and mining knowledge, and he was immediately accepted into the city's exclusive men's organization, the Denver Athletic Club.

Maggie had little time to fuss about high society, however. She joined many charitable and political organizations that worked for important causes, and she made countless friends both rich and poor. She was a founding member of the Denver Women's Club, which organized traveling art exhibits, provided art instruction and art supplies to public schools, and helped establish school libraries. She set up public health clinics and started community vegetable gardens to feed the poor. She even started an animal-rights group, a forerunner of the Humane Society. In 1893 she helped lead the fight for women's suffrage, doing her bit to give women in Colorado the right to vote in national elections, making it the third state in the union to do so.

Margaret Brown was a special champion for children. In 1900 she hosted a party for underprivileged children in the Brown Palace Hotel. Through Denver's Riverfront Project, she raised funds to support a playground and a summer school for five hundred needy children. Working with one of her friends, Judge Benjamin Lindsey, she helped to establish a juvenile court system in Denver, so that children and teens who committed crimes were no longer housed with adult criminals. And wherever she was at Christmastime, whether in Denver or on one of her many trips, she always sent a shipment of clothes and candy to the children in Leadville.

Maggie also continued her quest for knowledge. In 1901 she hired tutors to help her improve her grammar and writing skills, and she later traveled to New York to study literature, drama, and foreign languages at the newly opened Carnegie Institute. The Brown family traveled a good deal, and Maggie enjoyed learning about languages and cultures from all over the world. She eventually learned to speak French, German, Spanish, Italian, and Russian.

Over the years, as she traveled around the world, Maggie picked up various skills in the different countries. In Paris, she took acting lessons from the same tutor who taught the great actress Sarah Bernhardt. She learned to yodel in Switzerland, to play classical guitar in Spain, and to play the ukulele in the tropical islands. Upon her return home from these trips, Maggie entertained her friends with her newfound knowledge, often while dressed in a Japanese kimono or other native garb.

Maggie loved to give parties, dinners, and fundraising events, though no one among the Sacred Thirty-Six ever attended them. In spite of this rejection, Margaret Brown was very popular, and her home, Lions House, was considered by many to be the social hub of Denver. At one point the *Denver Times* reported, "Mrs. Brown's vivacity and merry disposition is a most refreshing trait in a society woman of her position.... Mrs. Brown's gowns are as original as her

The fashionable Margaret Tobin Brown, early 1900s
—Courtesy Western History Collection, Denver Public Library

ideas and that's interesting, too." On the East Coast, where Maggie often vacationed and later lived, she was readily accepted by the social elite, counting worldly millionaires such as the Astors and the Vanderbilts among her friends.

In January 1903, Daniel Tobin's wife, Mary, died, leaving four young children, aged five to eleven. Maggie took her three nieces, Grace, Florence, and Helen, into her home and raised them with her own two children, who were in their early teens. She also maintained a close relationship with her nephew, Frank, who lived with other relatives nearby. In spite of her new responsibilities in caring for five children, she continued contributing her time to charitable and political causes.

J.J. shared his wife's generous nature. He helped members of Maggie's extended family by finding them jobs in his mines. In 1905 he and his associates bought and donated land for the construction of Denver's Cathedral of the Immaculate Conception. Margaret held a special fundraiser to help the church's building fund. The event, called the Carnival of Nations, was arranged to resemble a world's fair, with booths and exhibits representing countries from all over the world. It was a huge success. Maggie's organizational talents were widely recognized. In anticipation of one of her events, a newspaper wrote, "With Mrs. J. J. Brown's indomitable pluck and energy at its head, it is certain to be a great social and financial success."

As Maggie continued with her many activities, J.J. spent more and more time on business and less time at home. Mr. and Mrs. Brown began to travel in separate circles. At this time, J.J.'s health was beginning to fail as well. He traveled to Arizona and California, hoping the desert climate would improve his health, while Maggie bought a home in Newport, Rhode Island, and began to spend a lot of time there.

In 1909 the Browns got a legal separation, though, because they were Catholic, they never got a divorce. In their settlement agreement, Maggie kept the house and the art collection and received $700 a month in support from her husband. By this time, the Brown children were grown, and two of Daniel's three girls were teenagers. Maggie often brought her nieces with her to Newport and on other trips.

In January 1911 Maggie's son, Larry, age twenty-two, got married and began working in the mines in Cripple Creek. By the end of the year, Larry and his wife, Eileen, had a baby boy, Lawrence Junior, whom the family called Pat. Maggie was delighted to be a grandmother. Later that year, Eileen took the baby to Kansas City to stay with her mother.

In the spring of 1912, Maggie and her daughter, Helen, took a trip to Egypt, Italy, France, and England. They were touring with tycoon John Jacob Astor and his wife, among others. While abroad, Maggie received news that her grandson, little Pat, was very ill in Kansas City. She immediately bought two tickets to New York City on the maiden voyage of a British luxury liner, the *RMS Titanic*. At the last minute, Helen decided to remain in Europe, so Maggie, accompanied by the Astors, embarked without her on April 10, 1912. In addition to personal baggage, Maggie took onboard several crates of Egyptian artifacts she had collected abroad for the Denver Art Museum.

The *Titanic* had been much ballyhooed as the latest in nautical technology and was advertised as the world's fastest and safest ship. It was nearly 900 feet long and weighed over 46,000 tons. When it left on its maiden voyage across the Atlantic, it was carrying 2,235 passengers and crew. Its captain, Edward Smith, was about to retire, and this was intended to be his final voyage for the company. Word was that he intended to set a speed record.

With the voyage well under way, everyone was enjoying the lovely luxury liner when, on the night of April 14, the vessel struck an iceberg in the North Sea. (Whether or not this happened because the captain was going too fast is the subject of much debate among historians.) At first, although the ship had sustained damage, no one thought it would sink. It soon became clear, however, that the *Titanic* would not last the night.

When the ship hit the iceberg at 11:35 p.m., Maggie was in her stateroom reading a book. She wrote in her journal, "So completely absorbed in my reading, I gave little thought to the crash that struck at my window overhead and threw me to the floor." When she went outside to investigate, she met a man who gasped, "Get your life-saver!" and told her to go out to the lifeboats on the lower deck. She hurried to put on the warmest clothes she had. Along with a velvet suit, she donned several pairs of stockings, a sable fur coat, and a silk cap. Before grabbing her lifejacket and leaving the cabin, she quickly tucked $500 in cash into her pocket along with a small Egyptian figurine for good luck.

At the lifeboats, confusion reigned. Maggie learned that there were not enough boats for everyone onboard; women and children were instructed to go first. She wanted to stay and help, but two crewmen took her by the arms and hoisted her into Lifeboat Number Six as it was about to be lowered into the sea. This boat could have carried sixty-five people, but in the chaos, only about twenty-four, mostly women, were aboard when it was launched into the water.

Those onboard Lifeboat Six rowed as hard as they could away from the ship to avoid being sucked under as the *Titanic* sank. Their view of the starboard side of the vessel showed that the E and C decks were already under water. Maggie watched in horror as the ship went down, later writing, "Suddenly there was a rift in the water, the sea opened up, and the surface foamed like giant arms that spread around the ship."

Maggie argued with the quartermaster, who was in charge of the lifeboat, to turn back to look for survivors, but he refused, as-serting that everyone in the water was already dead. An enraged

Maggie threatened to push him overboard. The man backed down, and Lifeboat Six rowed back, searching the waters for signs of life, but they found none.

Adrift now in the small lifeboat on the dark, icy sea, Maggie took charge. She did her share of rowing and encouraged the others, leading them in songs to keep up their spirits. She took off some of her extra clothing and gave it to others who were freezing in the boat. The passengers in Lifeboat Six rowed for many hours in the bitter cold before they were picked up by the *Carpathia*, the nearest ship to hear the distress signals from the *Titanic*, early in the morning. Maggie's lifeboat was the last one picked up in the rescue.

Once aboard the *Carpathia*, Maggie continued to work tirelessly to help others. Her knowledge of languages helped her assist the rescued passengers who did not speak English. She paid for telegrams sent from the ship to survivors' worried friends and relatives. She even organized a survivors' fund for medical expenses and temporary lodging for those who needed it. By the time the *Carpathia* docked in New York, she had already raised $10,000.

"I was the most fortunate woman on the boat," Maggie told the reporters who flocked around her as she stepped off the ship. "Although I lost my worldly possessions, I lost no dear ones and I was healthy." Upon her arrival in New York, she was overjoyed to learn that her baby grandson had recovered (he would live to be sixty-five), though with all the commotion she had to postpone her plans to go see him. Even though she was eager to go home, Maggie returned to the *Carpathia* for an extra day to help some immigrant women who had no money and no place to go.

About two-thirds of the *Titanic*'s passengers and crew perished in the tragic accident, and very few bodies were recovered. Of more than 2,200 people aboard, only about 705 survived. At the time, it was the worst peacetime shipwreck of the twentieth century, and it came to be one of the most famous (or infamous) maritime disasters of all time. In addition to the lives lost, significant artwork went down with the ship, including Maggie's collection for the Denver Art Museum and an ancient book of poems in a jewel-encrusted binding. Inquiries into the wreck led to sweeping reforms in Great Britain's shipping industry.

By the time she got back to Colorado on April 29, Margaret Brown was famous. When she stepped off the train in Denver, she found a crowd waiting to greet her. Maggie's family and friends were overjoyed to see her. A few days later, none other than the Sacred Thirty-Six welcomed her back to Denver with a luncheon given in her honor at the home of Mrs. Crawford Hill.

Maggie was a bit overwhelmed by all the attention. In a letter to her daughter she wrote, "I have had flowers, letters, telegrams, people until I am befuddled. They are petitioning Congress to give me a medal. If I must call a specialist to examine my head, it is due to the title of Heroine of the Titanic."

A ceremony was held in New York on May 29, 1912, to honor the captain and crew of the rescue ship *Carpathia*. The captain, Arthur Henry Rostron, was awarded a gold medal and a silver trophy; the crewmen were also awarded medals. Margaret Brown was one of the presenters at the event. She personally presented Captain Rostron with the Egyptian good-luck charm she had taken with her before she abandoned ship. Years later, Maggie helped organize the creation of a monument to memorialize those who died in the *Titanic* disaster. The thirteen-foot-tall granite statue was unveiled in Washington, D.C., in 1931.

When Congressional hearings were held to investigate the wreck, Maggie was infuriated to learn that she was not allowed to testify because she was a woman. She wrote her own report and had it published in major newspapers worldwide.

Once the furor over the *Titanic* disaster settled down, Maggie went back to her good works. She decided she could use her new fame to good advantage by speaking out on issues she cared about. Back in Colorado, one event particularly captured her attention. In September of 1913 in Ludlow, more than 1,000 coal miners went on strike. After the strikers were evicted from their company housing, they put up a tent city and stayed there for months. The mining companies continued to refuse the union's demands, and a series of violent incidents followed. Finally, in April 1914, the National Guard was sent in. The militiamen set the workers' tent city on fire, killing at least nineteen people, including eleven children. The incident became known as the Ludlow Massacre.

Maggie Brown well remembered the hard conditions of the miners and their families in Leadville. She was quick to respond to needs in Ludlow, sending first-aid supplies, clothing, and shoes and raising funds for further assistance. She also intervened on the miners' behalf to help settle the strike and to investigate the massacre.

Later in 1914, encouraged by her friends, Margaret Brown considered a run for Congress. She had support in Colorado for her earlier efforts on behalf of women's suffrage and for her other good works. She believed she would have backing from Democrats and Progressives.

Yet many people opposed Maggie's political ambitions. More than a few felt that a woman had no place in government—nationally, women had not even won the right to vote yet. Newspapers suggested that even if she were elected, Congress would not seat her. Yet Maggie was determined. In an interview with the *New York Times*, she said, "If I go into this fight, I am going to win. . . . That I should be mentioned as a possible candidate for United States Representative from my home state—Colorado—is glory enough for any one woman. There is only one greater glory—to *be* that representative."

Maggie's campaign was already losing momentum when world events changed the game on the political landscape. World War I was about to begin, and conditions in Europe became frightening.

Thinking it best not to challenge legislators already in office, Maggie dropped out of the Congressional race. The fact that her sister Helen had recently married a German nobleman undoubtedly had something to do with Maggie's decision, since Germany was about to become an enemy of the United States. Publicly, however, she gave only one reason: "I believe those in Congress might be permitted to remain to finish the important business there, especially as war is on in several European countries."

The war in Europe broke out in July 1914; America sided with Great Britain, France, and their allies but would not officially join the fight until April 1917. Leaving her political ambitions aside, Maggie dedicated herself to activism on the home front. She had plenty of work to do. She traveled to France with an American relief committee that had been formed to assist the war-ravaged French people. She also worked with the Red Cross in France, and she later turned her Newport home over to the Red Cross to be used as a hospital.

After the war, Maggie moved to New York, where she devoted time to helping soldiers who had been blinded in battle. In 1932, in recognition of these and numerous acts of benevolence, Margaret Brown received France's highest award—the French Legion of Honor.

In the fall of 1922, J. J. Brown died in a Long Island hospital after suffering several heart attacks. He had left no will. Although J.J. and Maggie had been separated for years, she was still his legal wife, causing considerable confusion in the distribution of his estate. The two children, Larry and Helen, felt that their mother wanted more money than she was entitled to. Just before J.J.'s death, a large sum had been transferred to Helen to buy a house, and Maggie questioned this. Eventually the matter was settled—Maggie got approximately half of the estate, and Larry and Helen received one-fourth each—but the rift that had developed between Maggie and her children because of the money had ruined their relationship for good.

Maggie eventually returned to Denver, moving back into the House of Lions, but she continued to travel extensively. On a trip to Palm Beach, Florida, in 1925, her courage and leadership was tested once again when a fire broke out in the hotel she was staying at. Just as she had taken charge in Lifeboat Six, Maggie led a group of fellow hotel guests out of the building to safety. No lives were lost in the fire.

Although Maggie traveled the world over, she always remained attached to Colorado. In 1930 she bought and restored the Denver home of the poet Eugene Field, then donated it to the city to be used as a museum and library. Maggie's own house in Denver, the House of Lions, was made into a museum many years after her death, as was the Browns' summer home, Avoca Lodge. Today the Molly Brown House Museum and the Molly Brown Summer House are both major tourist attractions visited by several thousand people each year.

Maggie, who had studied acting in New York and Paris and appeared onstage in both cities, spent the last few years of her life as an actress in New York City. Off and on between 1929 and 1932, she lived in the Barbizon Plaza Hotel, near Broadway, and she continued to study acting and taught acting as well. It was while living at the Barbizon that she suffered a series of strokes, the result of a brain tumor. Margaret Tobin Brown died on October 26, 1932, at age sixty-five. She was buried at a cemetery in Long Island, next to J. J. Brown.

With her larger-than-life personality, Maggie Brown was a bit of a legend in her own lifetime, but she became an even bigger legend after her death. Over the years, various writers embellished her life story; for some reason, many of these writers referred to her as "Molly" Brown, and this was the name by which she would be remembered forever after.

In 1960 a musical comedy called *The Unsinkable Molly Brown*, loosely based on Maggie's life, became a hit on Broadway. The show, more fiction than fact, made Molly Brown a household name (even though it wasn't really her name). The play was soon made into a movie, which was also a hit, spreading the legend even further. Later books, movies, and television shows added to the confusion between the fictional character and this real-life heroine. But the myths are hardly more exciting than the truth about Margaret Tobin Brown—adventurer, activist, and altruist; socialite, suffragette, and survivor—a bold role model for the girls and women of yesterday and today.

*Emily Griffith, wearing hat made by a student
at the Opportunity School, circa 1913* —Courtesy
Western History Collection, Denver Public Library

"For All Who Wish to Learn"

Emily Griffith, the petite, red-haired principal of the Opportunity School in Denver, did not call her faculty together often. She wanted her teachers to focus on fulfilling the needs of their students, not on what she regarded as "adminis-trivia." When she did assemble her teachers for a meeting, she kept it short and to the point.

The year was 1918, and the Opportunity School for adult education had been open for two years. The message she delivered to her staff today was this: "No one in our school is supposed to frown. Any one of the staff who is heard to speak a harsh word is subject to immediate dismissal. Nor is a teacher permitted to call attention to a student's weaknesses. Many people have been ridiculed in other classrooms. Give a student an assignment in the beginning, an assignment that he can do, one that will be of importance to him. When that one is done, give him another assignment. Here we try to make them happy, believing that when they are happy, they are interested and want to learn. . . . We do not believe in failure."

Emily K. Griffith, a woman who was to make an enormous contribution to the field of adult education, was born in Cincinnati, Ohio, on February 10, 1868. She was the oldest of three girls (her sisters were Florence and Ethelyn) and had one older brother (Charles).

Even as a young girl, Emily carried considerable responsibility at home. Her mother, Martha, was frail and sickly, so Emily helped out a lot around the house. Her father, Andrew, who walked with a severe limp, had trouble supporting the family. Though Andrew was a lawyer for a while, he did not make much money at it. He moved his family often, which disrupted Emily's education. Emily's sister Florence was referred to as "feeble-minded"; she may have been mentally impaired or had an acute learning disability. She also suffered from epilepsy. Emily protected and looked after Florence throughout her life.

In 1884 the Griffiths moved to central Nebraska, where Andrew filed a claim on one hundred acres of land in Custer County. He wasn't very successful as a farmer, and though he supplemented his income as a justice of the peace, the job brought in little money. Emily's brother, Charles, age eighteen, earned a small income as a postmaster. For the family to get by, Emily also had to find work. At age sixteen, she decided to become a teacher.

Emily had only an eighth-grade education herself, but teachers were in short supply on the prairie, so the county school board called her in as an applicant. Recalling her examination by the board members, Emily recounted that she almost wasn't hired because one of the board members didn't like the way she formed the letter s. Her application was accepted, however, and after completing a two-week teacher-training course, she was granted a teaching certificate and assigned to a sod schoolhouse in a remote part of Nebraska. Some of her students were older than she was.

Most of the money Emily earned teaching went to support her family, but it wasn't much. As was commonly the case for teachers at the time, Emily wasn't paid enough to cover her own living expenses, so she stayed at the homes of her students, spending a week with each, then moving in with another family for the following week. Living in so many different homes, Emily noticed that the parents of the children she taught often could not read and write themselves. Many were immigrants from Germany, Sweden, eastern Europe, and elsewhere, and they were not always fluent in English. Her experiences with these hardworking but uneducated adults no doubt contributed to Emily's later dedication to adult education. If the parents could receive more education, she reasoned, the children would do better as well.

Weather on the Nebraska prairie could be challenging. Blizzards and subzero temperatures were common in winter, and spring sometimes brought tornadoes. One day a tornado struck Emily's schoolhouse while class was in session. When she saw it coming, Emily had her students line up in the center of the room, near a center support pole and away from the window. Sure enough, the twister hit, blowing the roof off and collapsing the walls, but none of the children were harmed.

Finding the Nebraska farm a struggle, Emily's family moved to Denver in 1894, hoping for more opportunities in a large city, and she went west with them. But the prospects in Denver were hardly brighter. Like most other U.S. cities, Denver was suffering from the economic depression that followed the national financial panic of the previous year. Many mines had closed and people had lost their jobs. By this time, Andrew Griffith had given up on both law and farming and had become an itinerant missionary. Driving a horse-drawn wagon, he sold Bibles and religious tracts, earning almost nothing. Mrs. Griffith was an invalid by then, so Florence kept house while Ethel attended school. Twenty-six-year-old Emily knew it was up to her to support the family. She hoped to teach school in Denver, based on her experience in Nebraska. She began as a substitute teacher before she was hired to teach sixth grade at Central School in Denver.

Over the next nine years, Emily proved to be an excellent teacher. In 1904 she was offered the position of Deputy State Superintendent of Schools under Katherine L. Craig. After serving in this role for four years, Emily said she missed the classroom and asked to return to teaching students. She was assigned to teach eighth grade at the Twenty-fourth Street School. The school was located in a poor neighborhood with high truancy. Emily took the time to visit many of her students' homes to convince their families to make sure the children completed their education. In 1909 she received a "complimentary state teaching diploma for excellent service," allowing her to teach in any school in Colorado.

After two years at the Twenty-fourth Street School, Emily was called back to again be the Deputy State Superintendent. She served in this capacity for another two years, visiting many classrooms and working to make improvements in the schools. During this period she also attended the Denver Normal School (teacher's college) for twenty-eight weeks. She returned to teaching eighth grade at the Twenty-fourth Street School in 1912.

Throughout her time in Denver, Emily was always trying to raise funds for her needy students and their families. She spoke with businessmen about vocational opportunities for students and their parents, and she often asked friends and charitable groups for donations of money, clothing, school supplies, and Christmas gifts. Gradually, Emily Griffith became known throughout the Denver area as an educational advocate. Her name was familiar to the American Red Cross, the Jewish Aid Society, the juvenile court system, and the Y.M.C.A.

After a few years, Emily came up with the idea of teaching night classes at the Twenty-fourth Street School. Many teenagers had to take day jobs to help support their families, forcing them to drop out of school. Many parents, too, needed more education, to help themselves out of poverty. At first she had difficulty persuading the school board even to put gas lighting in the old building so that her night students could see. They finally gave in, though, and Emily began teaching her evening "opportunity school" classes in addition to her regular daytime classes. She invited board members to visit a few of these night classes, and they were favorably impressed.

Not everyone agreed that free night school was a good idea, however. Many thought it would lower teaching standards, while others complained of the extra cost to taxpayers. Some even questioned Emily's own qualifications as an educator, since she lacked a college education. Few saw the need for public schools to accommodate working people. Emily was well aware of the criticism, but she was not discouraged. She had no intention of lowering standards; she was determined to make sure the night school's course offerings were as excellent as those in any other school. She was quoted as saying, "I want to make Opportunity School easy to get into, but hard to get out of."

In December 1915 the *Denver Post* led a clothing drive for the poor. Schoolteachers were encouraged to send needy families to the event to take whatever clothes they could use. Emily personally accompanied a group of students to the clothing giveaway. While there, she struck up a conversation with a *Denver Post* staff writer, Frances "Pinky" Wayne, telling her about the night classes at the Twenty-fourth Street School. Wayne was interested in the idea of a free school open to young and old, day and night, and began pushing the idea in her newspaper column.

With public support growing, in May 1916 the Denver Board of Education was finally convinced and recommended that the old Longfellow School be refitted with new lighting and windows to serve as a free "opportunity school," open day and night. They also recommended that Emily Griffith be appointed principal. There was one remaining obstacle: a new law had to be enacted to authorize and fund such a facility. After Emily and other education advocates lobbied the Colorado General Assembly, the new statute was passed on April 10, 1917. In the meantime, the plans for the school were implemented.

Emily put an advertisement in the newspaper saying: "Wanted—All boys and girls to come to the Opportunity School." To attract adults, she had businesses put notices about the classes in their employees' pay envelopes. Until the school opened, Emily had no idea how many students she would have, how many staff members she'd need, how many rooms would be necessary, or what supplies and equipment she would require. The school board had provided her with only one box of broken chalk.

On the first day of school at the Longfellow building, September 7, 1916, Emily arrived early. With her that first day were five assisting teachers. They hung a sign above the door that read: "Public Opportunity School—For All Who Wish to Learn." As students started to arrive, it became clear that enrollment would exceed Emily's expectations and that the students had come for all kinds of reasons. Immigrants wanted to learn English, some people came to learn math, and others were interested in trade skills such as metalwork or carpentry. Emily admitted them all.

By the end of the first week, 1,400 people, ranging in age from fourteen to eighty-two, had signed up for school. Among these were about a hundred who wanted to learn typing, but the school had only one typewriter! As each obstacle arose, Emily met it. She would beg and borrow to get supplies for her students. By the end of the first year, the Opportunity School had 2,398 pupils and a faculty of 38.

Emily selected her own teachers, with final approval by the school board. She hired not only professional teachers, but also experts from the community, especially for the vocational subjects. She might hire an old miner from the hills, for example, to teach a class in prospecting, and retired Western Union operators taught telegraph communication.

The Opportunity School was open thirteen hours a day, five days a week. Emily did not have an office of her own at the school;

instead, she placed a roll-top desk in the front hall, just inside the entrance, so she could greet everyone who came and went. Her assistant's desk stood right next to hers. Near them was a blackboard on which Emily wrote messages to the students each day. Sometimes the day's message would simply be, "You can do it!" One day, after students asked her about tardiness, which was often unavoidable for working people, she wrote, "Enter your classes whenever you can get here. We know you try to be on time."

Clearly Emily cared about the personal welfare of the students, not just their academic performance. At the end of the day, she often gave some of them a nickel for the streetcar, and she sometimes invited students to her home for a meal. On one occasion, she even hosted a wedding for a young Chinese couple.

One evening, not long after the school opened, a student fainted in class from hunger, and Emily realized that many of the students had to come directly from work, with no time to go home to eat and, often, no money for a meal at a restaurant. She came up with a solution: free soup. Every day, Emily's mother made a big pot of soup at her home, and Emily's sister Florence carried it to the school by streetcar. Emily and Florence set up a dining area in the basement, and Emily included a new sentence at the bottom of her daily message: "A bowl of soup is served in the basement from 5:30 to 7:30 free." To protect the pride of the needier students, she added, "This saves you time."

The soup program was a success. As many as two hundred bowls were served each night. At first, Emily and Florence personally washed all the dishes every night, though they eventually employed a woman to do this. One day a member of a women's club heard about the free soup and wanted to contribute. She arranged to have meat delivered to the school each day, and Florence began to come in each afternoon to make the soup on a stove in the basement, rather than carry it all the way from her mother's house.

HISTORICAL TABLEAU GIVEN BY THE ADVANCE OPPORTUNITY SCHOOL, FEB 21ST, 1

Soon the Opportunity School was occupying the entire building, and there was still not enough room for all who applied. The school was open to every Denver citizen, and the classes were tailored to meet the needs of the students, stressing trade and vocational courses. Business owners often excused their employees from work for several hours a week to attend classes to improve their skills. A bicycle room was set up in the school basement where Western Union messenger boys could park their bikes while they attended classes.

The curriculum was always evolving. Foreign-born adults learned to read and write in English and prepared for their citizenship examinations. Women came to learn cooking and crafts. With the advent of World War I, which America entered seven months

Opportunity School, 1918. Emily Griffith, in center with corsage, poses with students, some dressed in costume for a play
—Courtesy Western History Collection, Denver Public Library

after the school opened, the course program was expanded to offer instruction in using and repairing gas engines such as those used in wartime vehicles. Training for nurses, instruction in ambulance driving, and airplane mechanics were also added to the curriculum.

Soon a high school program was added for those who had no diploma. Many working people said they could not advance in their companies without a high school diploma; others simply wanted to expand their education. One young man, whose school records had been destroyed in a fire, was denied access to college, so he earned a new diploma at the Opportunity School. Another student, a seventy-year-old man, said that his diploma "gave him the right to express his opinion so that people would listen."

The school earned itself a good reputation, and Emily began to receive invitations to speak about the school or to set up similar schools in Germany, Great Britain, France, and Russia. Although she welcomed visitors from other places, she refused the offers to travel elsewhere, choosing instead to devote all her time to her own school and her own community. In 1922 she served as president of the Colorado Education Association.

In 1927 Emily founded a residence for homeless boys, now called the Emily Griffith Center, in Larkspur, Colorado. Around 1928 the Opportunity School became a sort of employment agency. Students seeking jobs put their names up on the school bulletin board, while employers with job openings posted "help wanted" notices. During the same period, Emily also began to work with the Denver police to start an educational program and halfway house for people just released from prison.

Emily's tireless efforts were in the Denver community, the state of Colorado, and nationally. In 1931 the *Denver Post* presented her with a merit award for her service to education and humanity and presented her with a special Colorado license plate number "1" for her car. The same year, the Business and Professional Women's Club named her Woman of the Year. Numerous articles about her and the Opportunity School appeared in national publications.

Emily announced her retirement in 1933. She was offered a nice pension, but she would accept only a small monthly allowance. By this time the Opportunity School, which had been operating for seventeen years, had served over 100,000 students. The following year, in honor of its founder and first principal, it was renamed the Emily Griffith Opportunity School.

After she retired, Emily moved from Denver to a rustic cabin in Pinecliff, Colorado, with her sister Florence and their cocker spaniel, Chips. Their other sister, Ethel, and her husband, Evans Gurtner, lived nearby. The little cottage had no electricity or indoor plumbing, and the sisters lived modestly on Emily's fifty-dollar-a-month stipend.

Although the place was somewhat remote, many people—teachers, students, friends—visited Emily there. Among the first to come see her was the new principal of Opportunity School.

Some people in the community were concerned about the now elderly Emily and her sister living in such primitive conditions. Some Denver businessmen offered to build them a new, better equipped home, but Emily politely refused the offer. Then one Sunday, some of her former students, many of whom were now successful in the building trades, came to the cabin and set to work putting in plumbing, electrical wiring, and other improvements. One of the volunteers' wives brought food, and before long, these "work on the cabin days" were treated as Sunday picnics, which continued long after the work was completed.

Even after Emily retired, she continued to receive awards, honors, and accolades. The Colorado Press Association presented her with the Eminent Service Award, a silver plaque, in 1939. Colorado Women's College conferred on her an honorary diploma in the humanities in 1942. And in June 1946, the Denver Kiwanis Club welcomed her as their first and only female member at a special program held at the Albany Hotel in Denver. Each member in turn praised her and presented her with a red rose. With an armful of roses, she gave a short, tearful speech of thanks.

Then on June 19, 1947, a horrible shock came to Denver. Newspaper headlines announced, "Emily Griffith, Sister, Slain in Cabin Home." The two women had been shot in the back of the head, murdered by an unknown assailant. No one could imagine who had done the heinous deed, or for what possible reason. Nothing had been stolen—indeed, there was little to steal. Later, an article about the mystifying murder even appeared in *Time* magazine.

In the early evening of June 18, Emily's sister Ethel had stopped by the cabin for a visit. When no one answered her knock, she figured her two sisters were out for a stroll, so she went home. Returning to the cabin the next morning, Ethel knocked on the door and even on the windows, but still no one answered. Alarmed, she hurried to get her husband, Evans, who had a key to the place.

Entering the cabin, Ethel and Evans found a horrifying scene: Emily lay dead in one bedroom, and Florence in the other. They called the police, who found no signs of a struggle or break-in. On the stove sat a pot of mashed potatoes and another of beans. Three slices of pie were sitting on the counter. It looked as if the sisters had been expecting a guest for dinner.

One name cropped up as a suspect, Fred Lundy. This man, who had retired as a teacher from Opportunity School many years before, was a close friend who lived nearby and helped the Griffith sisters with odd jobs, often eating meals with them. Lundy was missing, his cabin was locked, and his car was gone. Neighbors said Lundy had recently mentioned that he was leaving for a trip to Chicago. The car was soon found abandoned nearby. In it was a few hundred dollars in cash along with some papers about an inheritance for his niece and a note about where he wished to be buried. More than a month later, in August, Lundy's body was recovered from South Boulder Creek after two men stumbled upon it while fishing. Police ruled the death a suicide by drowning.

Did Fred Lundy murder the Griffith sisters, then kill himself? Even before his body was found, theories circulated that Lundy might have shot the women in a mercy killing, then committed suicide. The sisters were old and in poor health; perhaps Lundy felt he was doing them a favor. The day after the crime was discovered, a *Rocky Mountain News* headline asserted the dubious theory: "'Mercy' Motive in Killing Emily Griffith."

Neighbors reported that Lundy had been acting strangely and once said that he'd rather see them dead than living the way they did. Yet why would he choose such a violent method? Perhaps the murderer was just a deranged stranger who had happened by.

Some speculated that Evans Gurtner, the Griffiths' brother-in-law, was responsible, since his wife stood to inherit her sisters' estate, which, though modest, was still worth several thousand dollars. Even Ethel herself could have been involved. A satisfactory answer to the mystery has never been found, and it remains an unsolved case to this day.

The sisters' funeral, held at Central Presbyterian Church in Denver, was attended by hundreds of mourners. Emily and Florence were buried side by side at Denver's Fairmount Cemetery.

The tragic end to Emily Griffith's life does not overshadow the tremendous contribution she made to education in Colorado. In 1985 Emily was inducted into the Colorado Business Hall of Fame. And in 2000 Denver mayor Wellington Webb honored Emily with one of ten Millennium Awards, given to honor people who had "made the most significant and lasting contribution to the citizens of Denver." Furthermore, Emily is one of a few women to have a stained-glass image in the windows of the Colorado Capitol.

Of all her honors, however, the most fitting memorial to this great teacher is that the Emily Griffith Opportunity School still survives, covering more than an entire square block of the city of Denver. In 2011 the school, which now offers more than five hundred courses, changed its name to Emily Griffith Technical College to "better reflect its mission." Thousands of students continue to graduate each year.

*Dr. Justina Warren Ford, circa 1899, around the
time she graduated from Hering Medical College*
—Courtesy Black American West Museum

The Lady Doctor

It was October 7, 1902. A serious young African American woman named Justina Ford stood in front of the county clerk's office in Denver, Colorado, and requested an application for a medical license. After filling it out, Justina handed in the form along with the five-dollar fee. The clerk took the application and the fee, but he said he felt "dishonest" taking the money, since there was no future in medicine for her: she was a woman and she was black.

In fact, Justina Ford had just made history. She was now the first black female doctor in the state of Colorado. Having already practiced medicine in Illinois and Alabama, her Denver practice would flourish. During her long career, she delivered more than 7,000 babies in the Denver area.

Justina Laurena Warren was born to Melisia and Pryor Warren on January 22, 1871, in Knoxville, Illinois, just six years after the end of the American Civil War. Her mother, Melisia, had been born into slavery in Kentucky. Melisia and her first husband, Ralph Alexander, had three living children, Emma, Ralph Junior, and John. After Ralph died, Melisia married Pryor Warren around 1870. Justina was the couple's first and only child. A short time later, the family moved to nearby Galesburg, Illinois, where Justina and her half-siblings grew up and attended school.

Justina's mother worked as a practical nurse for white families in Galesburg. African Americans in the community at that time had little access to medical services, so when the "colored folks" in town were in need of medical help, they came often to the Warren home, seeking care at all hours of the day and night.

Like many young children, Justina liked to play "hospital," but she never played a nurse—she was always a doctor. Since she didn't know the names of real medicines or diseases, she'd invent them. She also spent time dissecting chickens and frogs to see how their bodies worked. As she grew older, Justina helped her mother in caring for sick neighbors at her home and out in the community.

As her determination to become a doctor grew, she realized that if she wanted a career in medicine, she needed a very good education. She was willing to work hard to attain it. At Galesburg High School, Justina took difficult courses and earned top grades. When she graduated in 1890, her dearest hope was to go to medical school. At the time, female doctors in the United States were rare, and black doctors equally so, but Justina was ready to break through any barrier.

Love, however, delayed the would-be doctor's plans. At age nineteen, Justina met a twenty-eight-year-old black minister from Chicago. Justina's mother, who was one of the founders of the Second Baptist Church in Galesburg, may have introduced them. Two years later, in 1892, Justina married the Reverend John E. Ford. In her personal diary, in the entry dated December 26, 1892, she wrote, "This is my last entry as a single woman for tomorrow I will stand before God, my family and friends, and marry Rev. John E. Ford, in the church founded by my mama in Galesburg. My dream of going to medical school will have to wait until John gets settled in his new church in Chicago."

Shortly after the wedding, the newlyweds made the move to Chicago. By the fall of that year, Justina had enrolled as a student at

Hering Medical College, specializing in gynecology, obstetrics, and pediatrics. Family members helped pay the expenses of her education. Her journal entry of September 14, 1893, stated, "The more I learn, the more my desire to help people grows."

Finishing her studies in June 1899, Justina received a degree in medicine and an Illinois medical license. Afterward she and John moved to Normal, Alabama, where Justina began a two-year internship at the state hospital and served as resident physician at Tuskegee Institute. After completing her internship, she found that prejudice against her was keen, and she could not find work in a hospital or clinic. But she persisted, setting up her own practice, in which she served mostly poor patients, both black and white, in Alabama.

Meanwhile, in the fall of 1900, Justina's husband received a new church assignment in Denver, Colorado, and he moved there. Because Denver was a young, western town, Reverend Ford hoped it would have more opportunities for him. Justina, however, stayed in Alabama. "[John's] congregation continues to grow," she wrote in her journal nearly a year later, in August 1901. "I miss him but could not leave my patients. I have just begun. There are so many indigent people who are in need of my services. . . . There are so many children waiting to be born. I love all my patients, but my favorites are the children."

Justina had been on her own in Alabama for two years, increasingly lonesome for her family and her husband, when in September of 1902, her mother died. This sorrowful event finally prompted her to close her practice in Alabama and join her husband in Colorado. "John says there is a real need for doctoring in Denver. He says there are so many people with little money that the white doctors refuse to treat them. I'll never understand that kind of thinking. God intended us to be brothers no matter what color the skin." She was eager to be reunited with John. "I miss my beloved so," she wrote.

As Justina found out when she applied for her medical license, the western frontier was not free of prejudice and discrimination. Even though she was granted a license to practice, her applications for membership in the Colorado Medical Society were repeatedly rejected because of her race. Without that membership, she could not join the American Medical Association and therefore was not allowed to work in any city, county, or state hospital.

Justina went to work with Dr. William Cottrell, a black physician with a private clinic in Denver. In 1903 she delivered her first Denver baby. When Dr. Cottrell retired in 1905, Justina took over his practice, specializing in obstetrics. Her patients referred to her as "the Lady Doctor." Most of her patients were African Americans and poor immigrants, who were routinely turned away from hospitals. Justina noted in her diary on April 5, 1905, "I took the same oath as the white rich men 'to do no harm, to heal the sick,' and yet they cause harm every day they turn their back on colored people."

As years passed, Justina continued in her commitment to her Denver patients, seeing them at her office or in their homes. She did not send out bills but took whatever payment they could give her in money, goods, or services. Items she received for her service included poultry, eggs, produce, and hand-woven blankets. She took what she needed and gave the rest to indigent families. Sometimes she was paid nothing at all.

Most of Justina's patients did their best to compensate her for her services. Some paid right away, while others paid over time. Justina recalled one instance in which she received payment for delivering a baby when the child was thirteen years old. By that time, the doctor had forgotten all about it, but the mother hadn't.

In attending her patients, Justina found herself called out day and night, in all weather, sometimes traveling to the outskirts of town on treacherous mountain roads. She never failed to go. In addition to providing medical care, she often bought food, clothing, or coal for her neediest cases. She also helped people in her neighborhood apply for government aid and directed them to private charities and church support. Her assistance enabled many poor families to survive. The dedication, compassion, and generosity of Dr. Justina Ford soon became legendary in Denver.

Justina's husband was equally committed to his church congregation. He was a popular minister and a dynamic leader. Membership in his Zion Baptist Church grew from 100 to 400 in the four years he served as its pastor. Justina was as active in her husband's church as her busy schedule allowed, serving on a variety of church committees.

In 1907 John Ford began looking for a new challenge. When he left for a trip to Europe, most people thought he'd soon return to Colorado, but he did not. Instead, he took a new church assignment in Jacksonville, Florida. John occasionally came back to visit Justina and his church friends in Denver, but he never moved back. Eventually the strain on their marriage became too great, and in July 1915, Justina and John Ford divorced. They never had children.

After the divorce, Justina lived in a nine-room brick house, purchased in 1911, in a minority neighborhood called Five Points. This would be her home for the rest of her life. Upstairs were her living quarters, and downstairs were her medical offices. Justina offered her medical services to anyone, regardless of race, religion, or ability to pay. Because she earned little serving the poor, she also took in a few boarders.

Despite her modest income, Justina maintained a professional demeanor at all times and always dressed well, wearing a nice dress and hat whenever she left the house. One neighbor recalled seeing Dr. Ford at the scene of an accident late at night. In spite of the late hour, she was wearing a dress and hat.

Most families in Five Points preferred home births to hospital births, especially since the hospital in Denver was reportedly poorly equipped and unsanitary. Many women also welcomed a female rather than a male doctor to deliver their babies. She was a petite woman with small hands who could often deliver a baby without the use of forceps. In these respects at least, Justina had an advantage. The people in the neighborhood knew that the Lady Doctor cared deeply about children, and many times Justina found newborns left on her doorstep.

Justina's practice grew. In addition to African American, Native American, and poor white American patients, she also treated large numbers of immigrants, many of whom spoke little or no English. In order to better communicate with them, Justina eventually learned to speak several foreign languages, including Spanish, Italian, German, Greek, and Japanese. "Blue, black, yellow, or green, that's the way I take them," she noted amiably in her diary.

In 1920 Justina met Alfred (Alf) Allen, a cook for the Burlington Railroad. A few years later they married, but she kept the last name of her first husband, since Dr. Ford was the name she was known by. Alf, eighteen years younger than she, took care of the household duties while Justina continued her practice.

Although she was very busy treating patients, Justina saved two hours a day, Monday through Saturday, for other things. During the "telephone hour," she phoned her recent patients to check on them and answer any questions they had. During her "quiet hour" she read medical journals to keep up with the latest treatments. Sundays she attended church and spent time with Alf. She always kept this schedule except during medical emergencies.

In addition to her office hours, Justina often made house calls, going to see her patients on foot or by horse-drawn buggy, bicycle, streetcar, or taxi. Because she was well known in the community, cab drivers usually didn't charge her for the ride. Nevertheless, and even though she did not know how to drive, sometime in the early 1920s Justina bought an automobile. Alf usually drove the car.

Although it was useful, the car turned out to be a fateful purchase. In November 1923, Alf was driving with Justina and her half-sister, Emma Alexander Carter, who was visiting from Galesburg, when the car was hit by a train. Alf and Justina recovered from their injuries, but Emma died.

Three years after Emma's death, two of her grown children, Eugene Carter and Eva Carter Bradley, moved to Denver with their families. They stayed with their aunt in her big house, and Justina was happy to have family around. When they reached adulthood, her two grandnephews, Gene Carter and Jack Bradley, helped her by driving her on her rounds. Justina herself had delivered Gene in 1928, and Jack, who came to Denver with his parents at age

Dr. Justina Warren Ford, circa 1928, holding her grand-nephew, Gene Carter, whom she had delivered
—Courtesy Western History Collection, Denver Public Library

seven, later became the first black member of the Denver Symphony Orchestra.

Although Justina was content and successful in her own practice, she was still outraged that as an African American she was denied access to hospital facilities in Denver. She persisted for decades in applying, without success, for admission to the various medical societies that would allow her to become a full-fledged, accredited member of a hospital faculty. In 1935 she was made an adjunct staff member, rather than a full member, at Denver General Hospital, meaning that she was subordinate to the other doctors and did not enjoy full privileges.

Although she served admirably in her community for nearly fifty years, it was only late in her career that Justina received any recognition in Colorado. It was not until January 3, 1950, when she was nearly seventy-nine years old, that Justina was allowed to join the Denver and the Colorado Medical Societies. While she graciously accepted her admittance to the medical associations, at this late date, she had no intention of joining the staff of a hospital. But as she noted in her journal, "I'll never tell the board members that. I make it a practice to build bridges, not burn them." It was, in any case, a moral victory: she had broken through a barrier against people of color in Colorado. The following year, she received the Human Relations Award from the Cosmopolitan Club, a social club of the University of Colorado in Boulder. Many other honors came her way, but only after her death.

On October 14, 1952, only a few weeks after delivering her last baby, Dr. Justina Ford died in her home at the age of eighty-one. It was estimated that during her career, she had delivered more than 7,000 babies in Colorado (averaging about one baby every three days). Her funeral services were held in the Zion Baptist Church, where she had worshipped regularly, and she was buried in Fairmount Cemetery. In her obituary, the *Denver Star* wrote, she was "a friend of all humanity. Being a doctor, she was also intensely sincere in her desire to preserve all mankind."

Decades after her death, Justina finally received some of the recognition she deserved. She was inducted into the Colorado Women's Hall of Fame in 1985, and in 1987 the University of Colorado chartered the Justina Ford Medical Society as a support group for black doctors in training. The Colorado Medical Society recognized Justina Ford as a Colorado Medical Pioneer in 1989, praising her as an "outstanding figure in the development and furtherance of health care in Colorado." And in 1992 she was among the one hundred Coloradoans honored by Historic Denver, Inc., for "significant contributions to the formation of the State and lasting impressions on its people."

In the mid-1980s, the house in which Justina lived and practiced medicine was scheduled to be demolished to make way for a parking lot. A citizens' group rallied to save it, receiving a loan from Historic Denver to move the two-story brick structure to a new location about a mile away. After being placed at its current site, the Ford home was listed on the Register of Historic Places in 1984. Supporters also raised funds for its restoration and conversion into a black-history museum. The Black American West Museum and Heritage Center held its grand opening on September 24, 1988. In addition to exhibits relating to Justina Ford, the museum has a section devoted to black cowboys and another to the Buffalo Soldiers. The center also houses the Ford-Warren Public Library.

Today, at the light-rail station across the street from the Black American West Museum stands a life-size bronze sculpture of Dr. Justina Ford holding a baby. The statue, sculpted by Jess E. DuBois in 1998, was created as part of a regional public-art project. It is a fitting tribute to this courageous and compassionate pioneer doctor, yet Justina Ford's true monument may be the women and African Americans who followed her into the medical profession. Through them, her legacy lives on.

Josephine Roche (undated) —Courtesy Western History
Collection, Denver Public Library

9

JOSEPHINE ROCHE

Denver's Joan of Arc

November 21, 1927, was a dark day in Serene, Colorado. Workers at the Columbine coal mine had been striking for higher wages and better working conditions, in sympathy with an ongoing, state-wide coal miners' strike that had closed down nearly every mine in Colorado. After five weeks, the coal companies and their government sympathizers were anxious to put an end to the strike, and Governor William H. Adams called the state police to Serene.

Just after dawn on November 21, about 500 miners, some accompanied by wives and children, gathered at the gate of the barbed-wire fence that surrounded the company-owned town of Serene, a name now rendered ironic. The strikers carried American flags and signs—but no weapons. After their request to be let in was refused, the miners stormed the gate. As the strikers poured in, the militiamen fired on them, killing six and wounding about sixty others.

That night, 2,000 miners gathered in a nearby town and vowed to continue the strike. But they did not know what to expect. The major stockholder in the Columbine Mine, John Roche, had recently died, and his shares were now in the hands of his adult daughter, Josephine. Did she care about the killings? Would she listen to the miners' concerns? Would she do something to help them?

The answers to those questions, it turned out, were yes, yes, and yes. Within a few months, Josephine had secured a fair contract for the miners, ending the strike and earning her the nickname "Denver's Joan of Arc."

Josephine Aspinwall Roche, the only child of John and Ella Roche, was born in Neligh, Nebraska, on December 1, 1886. Her father began his career as a teacher but became an attorney, then a banker and investor, and eventually a conservative Republican politician. Ella was also a teacher when she met John in Wisconsin, and they married soon after. Sometime later, the couple moved to Nebraska, where John founded the Neligh National Bank, the London & Sioux City Finance Company, and the Omaha Cattle Loan Company. He also began investing in Colorado coal mines. From 1883 to 1885 he served in the Nebraska legislature as a representative and from 1889 to 1891 as a senator. By the time Josephine was born, the Roches were a wealthy family.

Since both of Josephine's parents had been teachers, and since they could afford it, they secured the best education possible for their only child. Josephine graduated from Brownell Hall, a private Episcopal girls' school in Omaha, in 1904. From there, she went to Vassar College in Poughkeepsie, New York. Two of her Vassar instructors had a considerable, long-lasting influence on her. Her history professor, Lucy Salmon, emphasized original research and debating skills; economics professor Herbert Mills taught social policy based on trade unionism. As a student, Josephine developed a progressive political philosophy, which stood in direct contrast to her father's beliefs.

While in college, in addition to her studies, Josephine took part in sports, debate, and other activities. She also joined an intercollegiate social-services organization called the College Settlements Association. One of her jobs was to monitor retail stores and their labor practices.

In 1906, while Josephine was still at Vassar, her parents moved to Denver, where John became president of the Rocky Mountain Fuel Company. Josephine began spending her summers in Denver working as an assistant with the juvenile court system under Judge Benjamin Lindsey (Margaret Brown's friend; see page 76). Her experiences at Vassar and in Denver inspired in Josephine a lifelong concern for children, immigrants, and the poor.

After graduating from Vassar in 1908, Josephine enrolled in the graduate social-work program at Columbia University in New York City. There she met another young social worker, Frances Perkins, who also strongly influenced her life. Frances would go on to become the first woman ever appointed to a Presidential Cabinet position, serving as Secretary of Labor under Franklin D. Roosevelt. Josephine, Frances, and ten other social workers lived in a settlement house, an experimental social-service program begun in the late nineteenth century where social workers lived among the people they assisted. Josephine's settlement house, Greenwich House, was in what was then a poor, largely immigrant neighborhood in New York's Greenwich Village.

For her master's thesis, entitled "Economic Conditions in Relation to the Delinquency of Girls," Josephine drew on her experiences with the troubled girls she met through Greenwich House and the Denver juvenile courts. Josephine believed in finding ways to reform young people rather than punish them.

Two years after she received her master's degree in 1910, Josephine was offered a job with the Denver Police Department and became the first female police officer in the city. Appointed "inspector of amusements," also known as a vice officer, she was in charge of policing neighborhoods for prostitution, gambling, illegal alcohol and drug sales, curfew violations, and other such activities. Josephine approached her new job with gusto, making regular inspections of dubious establishments, enforcing the curfew law for minors under twenty-one, reporting liquor violations, and shutting down broth-els. Her zeal angered many Denverites who profited from decadent activities and were accustomed to a more lenient attitude from the police. Among those who did not support Josephine's reform efforts were numerous corrupt city officials, including the mayor himself, Henry J. Arnold.

Nevertheless, Josephine remained committed to her campaign to protect young people from vice and corruption, enlisting the aid of newspapers to help spread the word about the dangers she observed. She particularly took up the cause of young prostitutes, often taking teenage girls off the streets and sending them home to their parents. Of the prostitutes arrested under her supervision, Josephine sent a large majority to the county hospital to be treated for gonorrhea, syphilis, or drug addiction. After hearing about this, Mayor Arnold ordered the hospital closed.

Josephine did not keep quiet about the corruption she saw in the city government. Among other things, she accused the president of the Police and Fire Board of letting his cronies sell liquor to minors. In February 1913, the reform-minded police commissioner who had hired Josephine, George Creel, was terminated. Two months later, Josephine found a note on her desk stating that she, too, was fired. As she later put it, "My activities in behalf of social betterment were obnoxious to the administration."

But Josephine refused to quietly accept her dismissal. Instead she filed suit against the city while continuing to work without pay. On July 8, 1913, a judge ruled that she had been improperly dis-missed and ordered that she be reinstated. Even though Josephine had won back her job, she faced so much hostility at work that she soon resigned. She then took a job as a parole officer in Denver's juvenile court system.

Over the next fifteen years, Josephine was active in a number of political and social causes, fighting for women's suffrage, civil rights, and labor reforms. Always interested in politics, she helped organize the Colorado Progressive Party and served as Colorado's only female delegate at the Progressive National Convention in Chicago in 1912. In addition to her longstanding concern for young people and immigrants, she also focused particular efforts on labor issues, including setting and enforcing safety standards for workers, instituting a minimum wage and an eight-hour work day, guaranteeing the right of workers to organize, and banning child labor.

In 1913 and 1914, Josephine witnessed the struggle of coal miners in southern Colorado to secure their right to organize. The fight between labor and management escalated to violence in April 1914, culminating in the infamous Ludlow Massacre, in which militiamen burned the strikers' tent village, killing thirteen women and children (see also page 83). Several miners were also killed in the melee. Enraged, Josephine rushed to Ludlow to assist the victims' families and take up their cause. She organized a group of widows and accompanied them to New York City, where they testified before the U.S. Industrial Relations Commission. The women's efforts and public pressure helped secure some basic reforms in labor conditions for miners and other workers in the United States, yet the battle for labor rights was far from over. While the next decade was a period of relative peace in labor-management relations, union protection was never secured.

In 1915 Josephine was recruited to become a special agent in President Herbert Hoover's Belgian War Relief Commission. World War I had begun in Europe, and though the United States had not yet entered the war, it was providing humanitarian support to allied nations. Early in the conflict, Germany had invaded Belgium and now occupied most of the country. The Allies had set up a blockade to obstruct supply lines to the German troops, but the blockade also prevented supplies from getting to the Belgian people, who were now starving. Hoover ordered his staff to organize a relief effort to bring aid to the Belgians via a canal through Holland.

Josephine trained for her new assignment in Fort Wayne, Indiana, before being sent to England, where she inspected the Belgian refugee camps in London. Back in the United States, she spoke at various gatherings to raise funds for the relief effort. A tireless worker, she visited forty-four American cities in one month, collecting money and foodstuffs for the cause.

After the United States declared war on Germany in April 1917, Josephine took a new job. As head of the newly created Division of Work with the Foreign Born, Josephine helped immigrants comply with American laws. Due to the war, many foreign-born people, especially those from Germany, Turkey, and other enemy nations, faced heightened intolerance and discrimination, and the government required that all immigrants sign registration cards and pledge their loyalty to the United States. Josephine set up nine foreign-language bureaus for immigrants to get information in their own languages. It was gratifying to her that during the war, only a very small percentage of immigrants were ever convicted of disloyalty to the United States.

At the end of the war, Josephine left her post at the government agency and founded the Foreign Language Information Service (FLIS) in New York City to help educate immigrants in their own languages. While working at FLIS, Josephine met journalist and dramatist Edward Hale Bierstadt. Edward was a staunch supporter of immigrant rights and other progressive causes, so he and Josephine appeared to have much in common, and they connected romantically. They got married on July 2, 1920. The marriage proved to be a short one, however, and they divorced in 1922. Edward married another woman four years later, but Josephine never remarried.

In 1923 the newly divorced Josephine moved to Washington, D.C., and became the director of the Editorial and Special Studies Division of the U.S. Children's Bureau. In this position, she worked for the passage of the National Child Labor Amendment and other legislation to help needy children and families. She also conducted national surveys about child welfare and published reports of her findings. After only two years at the Children's Bureau, however, Josephine resigned and returned to Denver because her father was ill.

While Josephine was a political progressive who supported workers' right to organize, her father, John Roche, held the opposite viewpoint. As an executive of the Rocky Mountain Fuel Company (RMFC), John did everything he could to break up union organizing in the coalfields. In spite of their radically different positions, however, the two remained very close.

John Roche died in January 1927. Six months later, Josephine's mother, Ella, also died. Josephine, now forty-one years old, inherited the Roche estate, which included considerable stock holdings in RMFC, the dominant company in the coal industry in northern Colorado.

By this time, labor relations in the Colorado coalfields were heating up again. After the failure of the 1913–14 strike in southern Colorado and the terrible Ludlow Massacre, union activities had been very low-key. A few miners joined the United Mine Workers union, but many were afraid to join for fear of losing their jobs. Yet coal miners still endured most of the same difficulties they did before—poor wages, long hours, and dangerous working conditions.

In the fall of 1927, the Industrial Workers of the World (IWW) called a statewide mining strike; almost all coal miners, whether union members or not, supported the strike. Soon nearly every coal mine in Colorado was shut down. Management in southern Colorado (Colorado Fuel & Iron) negotiated a settlement with the strikers, but in the northern part of the state, where most coal interests were owned by RMFC, the strike continued. By mid-November, the only coal mine still open in northern Colorado was the Columbine mine in Serene, where scabs (outside workers brought in to replace striking employees) kept operations running, though at reduced capacity.

When Josephine took charge of her father's mining interests, she tried to settle the problem. She dismissed a guard who had shot and killed a union organizer, and she appointed Merle Vincent, a reasonable man who was willing to negotiate, as general manager. Vincent immediately offered the strikers a wage increase, but the IWW urged them to reject the offer as inadequate. The strikers escalated their activities and several were arrested. Finally, Governor Adams stepped in, activating a unit of state rangers and sending them to the Columbine mine. Vincent, knowing that Josephine would strongly disapprove of having troops at the mine, called the governor, who tried to call off the rangers but failed to reach them.

The Rocky Mountain Fuel Company was housing the Columbine scabs in Serene, which was fenced off with barbed wire and protected by armed guards. Thus Columbine miners who lived in Serene were kept out of their own community. On November 21, some 500 unarmed strikers gathered at the gate and broke through the barriers. Failing to beat them back with clubs and tear gas, the guards, along with the state rangers, fired into the crowd, leaving six miners dead and dozens of other men and women wounded.

Josephine, outraged and sickened by the incident, rushed to Serene from Denver and immediately ordered the guards to disarm. Although she had some power in RMFC, her inheritance had made her only a minority stockholder. To settle the strike, she needed majority control of the Columbine mine. She took out a loan and bought more stock, enough to make her the majority stockholder.

In March 1928 Josephine promised the workers that if they organized in a union affiliated with the American Federation of Labor (she refused to work with the radical IWW), she would negotiate a union contract. Soon the miners had a new contract that raised wages to a record $7 a day and provided for an eight-hour day and a six-day week. It also guaranteed the formation of a grievance committee—a group of three miners who could meet with foremen to settle disputes. It was the first union contract in the coalfields of Colorado.

Josephine was praised in the newspapers for her humanitarian outlook. She believed that "What's good for labor is good for business." For a time this seemed to be true. With happier workers, production at the mine skyrocketed, and for a time, RMFC was the most profitable coal company in Colorado. But it was not that simple.

RMFC had debts, and bankers that had lent money to her father would not lend to Josephine. Then the Great Depression hit. Coal sales declined and prices dropped. As competing companies reduced their prices, they also reduced their workers' wages. Still RMFC survived, largely because of loyal union workers, who launched an advertising campaign for the company and agreed to lend the company money through a voluntary wage cut. Thus Josephine was able to keep the company limping along for a while. In 1934, ready to move on to pursue her other interests, she hired an excellent manager, J. Paul Peabody, to direct the company's finances and daily operations.

Leaving RMFC in good hands, Josephine again turned her attention to politics. The incumbent Democratic governor of Colorado, Edwin C. Johnson, appeared to be uninterested in many of the social-reform issues that were dear to her heart. In May of 1934, she challenged Johnson in the Democratic primary. Her decision came as a surprise to many. Running against an incumbent was a long shot, but Josephine said she was running to ensure "justice and fair play for the working men." In the September election, although Josephine won in Denver, the incumbent Johnson won in fifty-nine of Colorado's sixty-three counties. After losing the primary, Josephine did what any loyal Democrat would do and threw her support to Johnson.

Two years before, Josephine had campaigned for Franklin D. Roosevelt in his successful bid for president. She knew the First Lady, and her old Vassar classmate, Frances Perkins, had recently been appointed Secretary of Labor. After her loss in the governor's race, due to her connections with and support of the Democratic Party, Josephine was appointed Assistant Secretary of the Treasury in November 1934. She was only the second woman in history to hold a subcabinet post.

Josephine's new position entailed many significant responsibilities. She oversaw the Treasury Department staff and represented the department on the president's Cabinet Committee on Economic Security. She arranged financing for several of Roosevelt's New Deal programs, including the Social Security Administration, and was appointed head of the National Youth Administration. She also served as spokeswoman for the president's public health policies.

After only three years in her Treasury position, however, J. Paul Peabody, the man Josephine had appointed director of the Rocky Mountain Fuel Company, unexpectedly died. Josephine resigned from her job in Washington and returned to Denver. Although Peabody had done a good job managing the company, it was nevertheless struggling. The economy was still in poor shape, and increased competition from natural gas was cutting deeply into coal sales. In addition, the coal reserves in the company's mines were becoming depleted. Finally, in February 1944, after keeping the RMFC afloat through a major depression and a major war, Josephine filed for Chapter 10 bankruptcy. The last Rocky Mountain Fuel Company mine, the Columbine, closed its operations in 1946.

In 1939, while Josephine was still dealing with RMFC, President Roosevelt sent her to Cuba to represent the United States at the International Labor Organization Conference. At the 1945 conference, which met in Paris, President Truman sent her to serve again in the same capacity. Then in 1948, when she was sixty-two years

Josephine Roche with labor leader John L. Lewis, late 1930s
—Courtesy Colorado Historical Society

old, Josephine accepted another new position. John L. Lewis, president of the United Mine Workers of America, hired her to work on the newly formed Mine Workers Retirement and Welfare Fund, of which she soon became executive director. As fund director, Josephine testified before Senate committees, prepared reports, and guided the multimillion-dollar fund through tumultuous economic and political times.

After the United Mine Workers fund was dissolved in 1970 and her position was eliminated, Josephine kept busy. Now in her eighties, she returned to Colorado to organize her papers, most of which she donated to the University of Colorado. When asked by a reporter if she was planning to write her autobiography, Josephine replied playfully, "Who in the hell would want to read it?" Besides, she didn't have time. "I'm going to do things now," she said. "I'm afraid I didn't fight hard enough." She spent her final years in Washington, D.C.

During her long career, Josephine Roche received numerous honors and awards. She was awarded honorary degrees from four different colleges and universities, including the University of Colorado. In 1935 she received the U.S. Steel National Achievement gold medal and, the same year, was named the nation's best businesswoman by the Denver Chamber of Commerce. She was listed as one of the Ten Most Outstanding American Women in 1936 and in 1941, and she received the Albert Lasker Award from the American Public Health Association in 1956. Eleanor Roosevelt called her "one of America's great women." Posthumously, Josephine was inducted into the Colorado Women's Hall of Fame in 1986.

On July 29, 1976, just four months short of her ninetieth birthday, Josephine Roche died at a hospital outside Washington, leaving no heirs. What this remarkable woman left was a legacy of progress as she crusaded for the poor, the young, the immigrant, and the hardworking coal miner.

Mary Coyle Chase, circa 1940s —Courtesy
Western History Collection, Denver Public Library

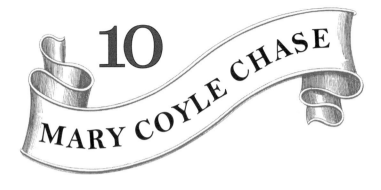

10 MARY COYLE CHASE

"Comedy without Malice"

The year was 1944; the place was the Forty-eighth Street Theatre in New York City. It was a preview performance of a new play, a comedy entitled *Harvey*. The playwright, Mary Coyle Chase, stood nervously in the lobby as the audience filed in. Her first two plays had not been well received, and Mary was haunted by doubt. What chance did this production have? Its title character was a six-foot-tall invisible rabbit.

Her expectations couldn't have been too high, because rather than spending money on a fancy dress for the opening, Mary borrowed one. In her purse she found a note from her husband that read, "Don't be unhappy if the play does not succeed. You still have your husband and your three boys, and they all love you." A heartwarming message perhaps, but not exactly a vote of confidence. As Mary took her seat, she was prepared, as much as anyone could be, for another flop.

But Mary Chase was in for a pleasant surprise. The audience absolutely loved *Harvey*. Not only did it become a big hit on Broadway, one that would run for nearly five years, but *Harvey* would also win Mary Chase a Pulitzer Prize—the first ever awarded to a Colorado writer.

Mary Agnes Coyle was born in Denver on February 25, 1906. Her home, near a large industrial area, was on the "wrong side of the tracks." She was the second daughter of Frank Bernard Coyle, an Irish salesman for the Hungarian Flour Milling & Elevator Company, and Mary McDonough Coyle, also an immigrant from Ireland. Mary Agnes was the youngest of the Coyles' four children. Her brothers were called Charlie and Frank (Junior); her sister was named Katherine.

Mary McDonough had come to America when she was sixteen to look after her four older brothers, all of whom had come to Colorado to prospect for gold, and none of whom was successful. She later met Frank Coyle, a recent arrival in Denver, and the couple wed around 1894. After the marriage, the McDonough brothers— Timothy, James, John, and Peter—were frequent visitors at the Coyle home.

Young Mary's mother and uncles often told her Irish folktales about fairies, banshees, and leprechauns as well as pookas, which are spirits disguised as animals and are visible only to those who believe in them. Mary's older brother Charlie also entertained her with his jokes and clowning (in fact, Charlie grew up to be a professional circus clown). Stories were abundant in the Coyle household, but money was not. Mary's mother helped stretch the family budget by sewing most of the children's clothes—their underwear was sometimes made from flour sacks.

Early on, although she was a bit of a tomboy, Mary showed an avid interest in reading, writing, and theater. She was even known to skip school occasionally to watch a matinee in Denver's exciting theater district. The first play Mary ever saw was a matinee performance of *Macbeth* at the Denham Theater.

An advanced student, Mary graduated from West High School at age fifteen and in the fall entered the University of Denver, where she studied Greek and classic literature. Her mother had scrimped and saved to set aside enough money for her daughter's tuition. After two years of college, seventeen-year-old Mary persuaded the city editor of the *Rocky Mountain News* to give her a summer job as an apprentice reporter. It paid nothing but gave her valuable work experience.

Mary then transferred to the University of Colorado in Boulder, which she attended from 1924 to 1925. It was a great disappointment to her that she was not invited to join a sorority. She left school before her senior year, returning to Denver in 1925 to take a full-time job writing for the *Rocky Mountain News*, where she earned fifteen dollars a week. She loved the rowdy world of journalism and spent a lot of time at the Denver Press Club with people such as photojournalist Harry Rhoades and columnist Lee Casey. Mary was a versatile writer. She covered news stories, wrote for the society page, and reported on boxing matches.

Mary became an intrepid reporter. On one occasion, she wanted to cover the completion of the Moffat Tunnel, but due to superstition, women were not welcome underground, so Mary was denied permission to go the ceremony. Undeterred, she disguised herself as a man, went to the forbidden site, and got her story. Another time, in order to get a story about a mine explosion, Mary flew in a small plane to reach the site. Suddenly the plane's engine died, forcing the pilot to make two desperate dives to avoid crashing. The sputtering engine finally caught, averting disaster.

Mary soon earned a reputation as a dedicated reporter who could write about anything from a society garden party to a street brawl. For the most part, she was accepted in the newsroom as "one of the boys." She once described a typical day of work traveling with photographer Harry Rhoades in his Model T Ford: "In the course of a day, Harry and I might begin at the Police Court, go to a murder trial at the West Side Court, cover a party in the evening at Mrs. Crawford Hill's mansion, and rush to a shooting at 11 p.m."

Yet Mary had a playful side. She liked to dress in the "flapper" style of the day and frequently attended fashionable parties. As a woman-about-town, Mary formed friendships with other women writers including Helen Marie Black, Greta Hilb, Margaret Havey, and Caroline Bancroft. She and Bancroft once gave a party for famed poet and wit Dorothy Parker, who was visiting from New York. The party attracted so many people that it caused a gigantic traffic jam. Police were finally called to end both the traffic jam and the party.

In 1926 journalist Robert (Bob) Lamont Chase joined the staff of the *Rocky Mountain News*. Bob and Mary became acquainted and

Young newswoman Mary Coyle (far right) hobnobs with royalty at the Brown Palace Hotel in Denver, 1926. (Left to right, Prince Nicholas and Queen Marie of Romania, Governor and Mrs. Clarence Morley, Henry Wollcott Toll, and Mary Coyle) —Courtesy Western History Collection, Denver Public Library

began dating. The couple married on June 7, 1928. Mary worked for the paper for another few years before she quit to raise a family and write plays. Mary had her first son, Michael, in 1932; another son, Colin, was born in 1935; and her third son, Barry Jerome (Jerry), came along in 1936.

Although money was tight, Mary found ways to get what she wanted. To pay for portraits of her three sons, she made a small payment every month for two years. On her way to apply for a loan, Mary once stopped to buy a new hat, which she could not really afford, because she felt she needed to make a good impression at the bank.

Although she was a busy young mother, Mary still did freelance reporting for the International News Service and the United Press. She later brought in a little money writing a weekly radio program for the Teamsters Union and doing publicity for the Teamsters and the National Youth Administration in Denver. In 1936 she and Bob helped found the Denver chapter of the American Newspaper Guild.

In addition to all this, Mary began writing plays. In the beginning, she found she had trouble getting her characters on and off the stage. To solve this problem, she built a miniature stage and used spools of thread to represent the different characters. Moving the spools on and off the stage, she was able to figure out the characters' movements in each scene.

Mary's first play, originally called *Me Third*, was written in 1936, around the time her third son was born. The play, a satirical farce that poked fun at political leaders, was first produced by the Baker Federal Theatre in Denver. A hit in Denver, the play was picked up to be produced on Broadway the following year. Under a new title, *Now You've Done It*, the show proved to be a flop in New York, closing after only forty-three performances.

Mary's second play, *Chi House*, was written in 1938. Based on her experience of being rejected by sororities at the University of Colorado, it is probably Mary's most autobiographical play. Produced at the University Civic Theatre at the University of Denver, it never played on Broadway, but the script was sold to RKO Productions and made into a movie, renamed *Sorority House*, released in 1939.

Lacking a major critical or commercial success, Mary decided to stop writing full-length plays for Broadway for a while, though she wrote a few one-act plays for university productions. This was the case with her next two plays, *Too Much Business* (1940), which portrays a world seen through the eyes of children, and a short comedy called *A Slip of a Girl* (1941), which was performed in army camps around the Denver area.

Mary later claimed that she wrote her next play just for laughs, not for money, though it took her two years to write. Her inspiration came during World War II, as she watched her neighbor walking by. The neighbor was a widow who had recently learned that her only son had been killed in action in the Pacific. Mary wondered if she could write anything that would make this woman smile again. She set a goal to write a sunny comedy to brighten people's lives during those dark times. A short time later, Mary had a dream in which a psychiatrist was being followed by a large white rabbit. Remembering her uncles' whimsical Irish tales, she began to write her new play, originally called *The Pooka*. She later retitled it *The White Rabbit* before finally settling on *Harvey*.

With her first draft completed, Mary contacted New York producer Brock Pemberton, who had directed her play *Now You've Done It* in 1937. Corresponding with Pemberton, Mary made over a dozen revisions to the script before the deal was settled. Pemberton hired Broadway legend Antoinette Perry, for whom the Tony Awards are named, to direct the production, and Frank Fey, a well-known comedian of the era, was cast in the leading role, Elwood P. Dowd.

Mary herself envisioned that at some point, the rabbit would appear onstage. No one agreed with her, but she couldn't be persuaded otherwise. Finally, during an open rehearsal before a small audience, the producers had an actor dressed in a rabbit suit appear onstage during the play. The audience groaned. Apparently people did not want to see a man in a rabbit suit, preferring to imagine for themselves what Harvey looked like. Seeing this, Mary agreed that the rabbit should never be seen in the play.

Harvey officially opened at the Forty-eighth Street Theatre on November 1, 1944. Mary's husband Bob accompanied her to the premiere, and they were both surprised at the size of the crowd. The play was a smash hit. The next day, the Chases took the train back to Denver, amazed at the play's success. Tickets were being sold for three months in advance. The play would run for four and a half years on Broadway, a total of 1,775 performances, making it one of the ten longest-running shows in Broadway history. It also became a classic, staged hundreds of times over the decades and into the current century.

When it opened, audiences and critics alike marveled at the play. *New York Times* reviewer Louis Nichols wrote, "*Harvey* is quite simply one of the delights of the season." Over the years, many people voiced their love of this gently funny play, including stage and screen star Helen Hayes, who would play the female lead in a Broadway revival of the show in 1970. She said that *Harvey* was a masterpiece, "comedy without malice."

With *Harvey*, Mary Chase became a celebrity, hounded by people wanting interviews and photographs. She maintained that she was still the same, but people now treated her differently. Uneasy about her newfound fame, she described herself as suffering from the "failure of success." Friends and family noted that the success of *Harvey* changed Mary from an extroverted "life of the party" to a much quieter and more serious person. She stopped drinking and used her *Harvey* royalties to organize a rehabilitation center for female alcoholics called the House of Hope.

On May 7, 1945, Mary Coyle Chase became the fourth woman and the first Coloradoan to win a Pulitzer Prize for Drama, beating out Tennessee Williams's acclaimed play *The Glass Menagerie*. After Mary won the prestigious award, a play that she had written years before *Harvey* was resurrected and produced on Broadway in 1945. *The Next Half Hour*, a tragic drama based on her unpublished novel, *The Banshee*, failed in New York and closed after eight performances. Apparently the public wanted only *Harvey*.

Indeed, *Harvey* was produced in cities across the country and in Europe. It received a very favorable response in London and Vienna as well as in most American cities. The play finally came to Colorado in the summer of 1947. Performed at the Central City Opera House with the original Broadway cast, it was a big hit. In the years that followed, the play often returned to Denver, produced at the Elitch Theatre (see chapter 5), the Bonfils Theatre, and the Auditorium Theatre. It also continued to play in New York, with different comedy stars in the role of Elwood P. Dowd.

Mary made many trips to New York and to Europe to see performances of the play. Rather than sit up front, however, Mary preferred to stand at the back of the theater and "listen to the music of the audience laughing," she wrote. "I could stand, anonymous as a ghost, in the lobby between acts, and see the smiling faces of people I would never know, enjoying the play."

In 1946 the Chases moved into a new home in an elegant country-club neighborhood in Denver. They called it "the house that Harvey bought." Mary decorated the interior with expensive antiques and Oriental rugs and filled the garden with fountains and statues. She remained active in the Denver community, serving on the boards of the Bonfils Theatre and the Denver Center for the Performing Arts.

In the late 1940s, Universal-International Pictures bought the screen rights to *Harvey* for $1 million—at the time, the highest price ever paid for a play or book. Mary coauthored the screenplay. Released in 1950, the film starred the great Jimmy Stewart as Elwood P. Dowd, and Josephine Hull played Elwood's sister Veta. The movie version was as popular as the play. Hull won an Academy Award for her performance, and Stewart was nominated for his.

In 1951 Mary completed her new play, *Mrs. McThing*, written specifically for children. She tried the play out with kids in her neighborhood before she sent it off to New York. Mary's agent insisted on giving it a two-week run on Broadway for "children of all ages." Opening in February 1952, *Mrs. McThing* earned rave reviews. Instead of two weeks, the play ran for a year, with 350 performances. The New York cast included Helen Hayes and Ernest Borgnine. The show was nominated for the New York Drama Critics' Circle Award. *Mrs. McThing* was later staged at the Central City Opera House in Colorado, with the original Broadway cast, for a one-month run.

Mrs. McThing was not Mary's only success in 1952. Another play for young people, *Bernadine*, opened that fall at the Playhouse Theatre in New York. This show, too, had a very successful run. In fact, during one week in 1952, *Bernadine*, *Mrs. McThing*, and a revival of *Harvey* were all playing on Broadway at the same time. In 1957 *Bernadine* was turned into a successful movie starring Pat Boone.

Over the next decade, Mary wrote several more plays for adults, of which only one, *Midgie Purvis*, was staged on Broadway. Although it starred the acclaimed Tallulah Bankhead, the 1961 production of *Midgie Purvis* was not a big hit. Gradually Mary decided to focus almost exclusively on writing for children. In 1960 she received the Monte Meacham Award from the Children's Theatre Conference of the American Educational Theatre Association (AETA), a group organized to promote theater for children. Mary wrote that the AETA had been "a source of encouragement to me in my playwriting in this field." In addition to plays, she wrote two children's novels, *Loretta Mason Potts* (1958) and *The Wicked Pigeon Ladies in the Garden* (1968). The latter was nominated for the Dorothy Canfield Fisher Award for children's literature and was later reissued as *The Wicked, Wicked Ladies in the Haunted House*.

Mary was honored many times in her home state for her contributions to Colorado literature. In 1944, in recognition of *Harvey*, the Colorado Authors' League presented her with the William MacLeod Raine Award for Outstanding Accomplishment. In 1947 the University of Denver awarded her the honorary degree of Doctor of Letters. She was also named an honorary member of the Denver Woman's Press Club. After her death, Mary was inducted into the Colorado Women's Hall of Fame in 1985 and into the Colorado Performing Arts Hall of Fame in 1999.

On October 20, 1981, Mary Coyle Chase, age seventy-five, died of a heart attack in her Denver home. She was buried in Denver's Crown Hill Cemetery. In a final bit of fun, Mary and her husband had chosen a cemetery plot right next to the graves of a Jefferson County couple with the last name of Harvey.

Bibliography

GENERAL REFERENCE

Ayer, Eleanor. *Famous Colorado Women: The Colorado Chronicles*. Vol. 2. Frederick, Colo.: Jende-Hagan Book Corp., 1982.

Colorado Women's Hall of Fame. www.cogreatwomen.org/

Epstein, Vivian Sheldon. *History of Colorado's Women for Young People*. Denver: VSE Publisher, 1998.

Flanagan, Mike. *Out West*. New York: Harry N. Abrams, 1987.

Riley, Marilyn Griggs. *High Altitude Attitudes*. Boulder: Johnson Books, 2006.

Shirley, Gayle C. *More Than Petticoats: Remarkable Colorado Women*. Guilford, Conn.: Globe Pequot Press, 2002.

Wood, Richard E. *Here Lies Colorado*. Online preview. books.google.com/books/about/Here_lies_Colorado_fascinating_figures_i.html?id=vc-t1evy3AQC

CLARA BROWN

Baker, Roger. *Clara: An Ex-slave in Gold Rush Colorado*. Central City, Colo.: Black Hawk Publishing, 2001.

Bruyn, Kathleen. *"Aunt" Clara Brown: Story of a Black Pioneer*. Boulder: Pruett Publishing, 1970.

Katz, William Loren. *The Black West: A Documentary and Pictorial History of the African American Role in the Westward Expansion of the United States*. New York: Touchstone Books, 1996.

Lowery, Linda. *Aunt Clara Brown: Official Pioneer*. Minneapolis, Minn.: Lerner Books, 1999.

Lowery, Linda. *One More Valley, One More Hill: The Story of Aunt Clara Brown*. New York: Random House, 2002.

Turner, Janine. *Holding Her Head High: Twelve Single Mothers Who Championed Their Children and Changed History.* Nashville: Thomas Nelson, 2008.

ISABELLA BIRD

Barr, Pat. *A Curious Life for a Lady: The Story of Isabella Bird, a Remarkable Victorian Traveler.* Garden City, N.Y.: Doubleday & Company, 1970.

Bird, Isabella. *Adventures in the Rocky Mountains.* New York: Penguin Classics, 2007.

Bird, Isabella. *The Englishwoman in America.* Madison: University of Wisconsin Press, 1966.

Bird, Isabella. *A Lady's Life in the Rocky Mountains.* Champaign, Ill.: Book Jungle, 2010.

DePorti, Andrea. *Explorers: The Most Exciting Voyages of Discovery from the African Expeditions to the Lunar Landing.* Buffalo, N.Y.: Firefly Books, 2005.

Encyclopedia of World Biography. "Isabella Bird." www.bookrags.com/biography/isabella-bird/

Hacker, Carlotta. *Explorers.* Women in Profile Series. New York: Crabtree Publishing, 1998.

Kaye, Evelyn. *Amazing Traveler Isabella Bird: The Biography of a Victorian Adventurer.* 2nd edition. Boulder: Blue Panda Publications, 1999.

McLoone, Margo. *Women Explorers of the World.* Mankato, Minn.: Capstone Press, 2000.

AUGUSTA TABOR

Bancroft, Caroline. *Augusta Tabor: Her Side of the Story.* Denver: Bancroft Booklets, 1961.

Coleman, Jane Candia. *The Silver Queen.* New York: Dorchester Publishing, 2009.

Kanzeg, David G. "Augusta Pierce Tabor." www.babydoe.org/augusta.htm

Karsner, David. *Silver Dollar: The Story of the Tabors.* New York: Crown Publishers, 1932.

Legends of America. "Rags, Riches, and Scandal: The Tabor Triangle." www.legendsofamerica.com/co-tabor.html

McMechen, Edgar C. *The Tabor Story.* Denver: State Historical Society of Colorado, 1959.

Moynihan, Betty. *Augusta Tabor: A Pioneering Woman.* Evergreen, Colo.: Cordillera Press, 1988.

CHIPETA

Becker, Cynthia. *Chipeta: Ute Peacemaker.* Palmer Lake, Colo.: Filter Press, 2008.

Becker, Cynthia S., and David Smith. *Chipeta: Queen of the Utes.* Montrose, Colo.: Western Reflections Publishing, 2003.

Krudwig, Vickie Leigh. *Searching for Chipeta: The Story of a Ute and Her People.* Golden, Colo.: Fulcrum Publishing, 2004.

Turner, Erin. *Wise Women: From Pocahontas to Sarah Winnemucca, Remarkable Stories of Native American Trailblazers.* Guilford, Conn.: Morris Book Publishing, 2009.

Whitley, Colleen, ed. *Worth Their Salt: Notable but Often Unnoted Women of Utah.* Logan: Utah State University Press, 1996.

MARY ELITCH LONG

Dier, Caroline Lawrence. *Lady of the Gardens: Mary Elitch Long.* Hollywood: Hollycrofters, 1932.

Faulkner, Debra B. *Mary Elitch Long: First Lady of Fun.* Palmer Lake, Colo.: Filter Press, 2008.

Gurtler, Jack, and Corinne Hunt. *The Elitch Gardens Story: Memories of Jack Gurtler.* Boulder: Rocky Mountain Writers Guild, 1982.

Hull, Betty Lynne. *Denver's Elitch Gardens: Spinning a Century of Dreams.* Boulder: Johnson Books, 2003.

MARGARET BROWN

Bancroft, Caroline. *The Unsinkable Mrs. Brown.* Boulder: Johnson Publishing, 1963.

Dannenberg, Julie. *Amidst the Gold Dust: Women Who Forged the West.* Golden, Colo.: Fulcrum Publishing, 2001.

Encyclopedia Titanica. "Mrs. Margaret Brown (nee Tobin)" www.encyclopedia-titanica.org/titanic-biography/molly-brown.html

Iversen, Kristen. *Molly Brown: Unraveling the Myth; The True Life Story of the Titanic's Most Famous Survivor.* Boulder: Johnson Books, 1999.

Landau, Elaine. *Heroine of the Titanic: The Real Unsinkable Molly Brown.* New York: Clarion Books, 2001.

Lohse, Joyce B. *Unsinkable: The Molly Brown Story.* Palmer Lake, Colo.: Filter Press, 2006.

Molly Brown Birthplace & Museum. www.visitmollybrown.com/

Molly Brown House Museum. www.mollybrown.org/

Rogoff, David. *Denver's "Unsinkable" Molly Brown.* Boulder: Stonehenge Books, 1980.

Ruffin, Frances. *Unsinkable Molly Brown.* New York: Rosen Publishing, 2002.

Simon, Charnan. *Molly Brown: Sharing Her Good Fortune.* Danbury, Conn.: Children's Press, 2000.

Whitacre, Christine. *Molly Brown: Denver's Unsinkable Lady.* Denver: Historic Denver, 1984.

EMILY GRIFFITH

Bluemel, Elinor. *Emily Griffith and the Opportunity School of Denver.* Englewood, Colo.: Privately published, 1954.

Bluemel, Elinor. *The Golden Opportunity: The Story of the Unique Emily Griffith Opportunity School of Denver.* Boulder: Johnson Publishing, 1965.

Emily Griffith Technical College. www.egos-school.com/site/public/history

Faulkner, Debra. *Touching Tomorrow: The Emily Griffith Story.* Palmer Lake, Colo.: Filter Press, 2005.

Lohse, Joyce B. *Emily Griffith: Opportunity's Teacher.* Palmer Lake, Colo.: Filter Press, 2005.

JUSTINA FORD

Cassidy, Jodie. *Reflections: The Voice of Pioneers.* "Remembering Colorado's First Female Physician: Dr. Justina Ford." PDF file. March 14, 2010. womenscollege.du.edu/voices/creativemedia/jodie_cassidy.pdf

Cox, Clinton. *Black Stars: African American Healers.* New York: John Wiley & Sons, 2000.

Lohse, Joyce B. *Justina Ford: Medical Pioneer.* Palmer Lake, Colo.: Filter Press, 2004.

Smith, Jessie Carney, ed. *Notable Black American Women.* Farmington Hills, Mich.: Thomson-Gale, 1995.

JOSEPHINE ROCHE

Conarroe, Carolyn. *Coal Mining in Colorado's Northern Field.* Lafayette, Colo.: Conarroe Companies, 2001.

Fong, Tillie. "Capitalist and Humanitarian." Colorado Millennium 2000. denver.rockymountainnews.com/millennium/0713mile.shtml

May, Lowell, and Richard Myers, eds. *Slaughter in Serene: the Columbine Coal Strike Reader.* Denver: Bread and Roses Workers' Cultural Center, 2005.

McGinn, Elinor. *A Wide-Awake Woman: Josephine Roche in the Era of Reform.* Denver: Colorado Historical Society, 2002.

Vassar College Encyclopedia. "Josephine Roche." vcencyclopedia.vassar.edu/alumni/josephine-roche.html

MARY COYLE CHASE

Alley Theatre. "Mary Chase, Playwright." www.alleytheatre.org/Alley/Mary Chase Playwright EN.asp?SnID=2

Chase, Tim. "There's Something About Mary." www.marycoylechase.com/Blog/Blog.html

Craig, Carolyn Casey. *Women Pulitzer Playwrights.* Jefferson, N.C.: McFarland & Co., 2004.

Ihler, Marlo M. "Mary Coyle Chase: Writing for the Human Spirit." Utah Shakespeare Festival, 2002. www.bard.org/education/studyguides/harvey/harveyplaywright.html

Sherwin, Mary, ed. *Comedy Tonight! Broadway Picks Its Favorite Plays.* Garden City, N.Y.: Doubleday & Co., 1977.

Wheatley, Christopher J., ed. *Twentieth Century American Dramatists.* Woodbridge, Conn.: Gale Group, 2000.

Index

Utes: 2, 43–54; Uncompahgre, 43–50
Ute language, 45

Vassar College, 114, 115, 122
vaudeville, 59, 60
Vienna, Austria, 62, 134
Views in the Far East, 28
Vincent, Merle, 120
Virginia, 6
Virginia (CSS), 64
Vitascope, 61

Wadsworth, Col. Benjamin, 9
Warren, Melisia, 103, 104
Warren, Pryor, 103
Washington, D.C.: Margaret Brown in, 82; Chipeta in, 42, 48, 49; Ouray in, 42, 47, 48, 49; Josephine Roche in, 118–19, 122, 124; Haw Tabor in, 39
Wayne, Frances, 93
Webb, Wellington, 101
Welk, Lawrence, 66
Welton, H. S., 52

Western Union, 94, 96
West High School, 128
White River Indian Agency, 43, 44, 52
The Wicked Pigeon Ladies in the Garden, 136
The Wicked, Wicked Ladies in the Haunted House, 136
Wilderness Road, 6
William MacLeod Raine Award, 136
Williams, Tennesee, 134
Windsor Hotel, 38, 39
Wisconsin, 114
women's suffrage, 74, 75, 83, 116
World War I, 83, 84, 96, 117
World War II, 132
Wurlitzer organ, 63

yaks, 26
Yangtze River, 28
The Yangtze Valley and Beyond, 28
Y.M.C.A., 92
Yokohama, Japan, 28

Zion Baptist Church, 107, 110

About the Author

Phyllis J. Perry is a graduate of the University of California, Berkeley. She received her master's degree from San Francisco State College and her doctorate from the University of Colorado, Boulder.

Phyllis grew up in a small gold-mining community in northern California, and after relocating to Colorado, where she has lived for more than forty years, she immediately felt right at home amidst the gold, silver, and coal mines of the Centennial State.

After serving in the Boulder Valley Public Schools as a teacher, curriculum specialist, principal, and director of Talented & Gifted Education, Phyllis retired early to write full-time for children and adults. She has published more than seventy books, including *A Kid's Look at Colorado* (Fulcrum Publishing, 2005) and the award-winning *It Happened in Rocky Mountain National Park* (TwoDot Publishing, 2008). She and her husband live in Boulder.